Galletti & Matter collection of places

buildings & projects

Birkhäuser – Publishers for Architecture
Basel • Boston • Berlin

Collection Archigraphy Lémaniques.
This collection, which simultaneously covers historical and theoretical fields, pursues the objective of publishing
the completed works of contemporary architects, and thus incorporating documentation for the founding of a critical
reflection relating to the evolution of architectural practice in Switzerland.

Collection Archigraphy Lémaniques is directed by Bruno Marchand.

Contents Pages

Spirit of materials

A visit to an architectural practice often holds many surprises. Particularly for those who seek to understand, in all its complexity, the work of an architect or a duo of architects from the initial concept through to the principles by which their creative working space is organised.

An office visit allows the privileged observer to dwell on a number of clues such as the arrangement of the room, its general layout, the images on the walls, the presence (or not) of models on the tables, etc.

This brings to mind the striking sight of Le Corbusier's office in the old convent in the Rue des Sèvres, where his employees worked at drafting tables arranged in a regimented, monastic row, a manifestation of the master's austerity and his need for control. Also, even more impressively, the offices of Eero Saarinen, cluttered with gigantic models that allowed him to achieve a better understanding of form, space and light in his projects.

When I first visited the offices of Olivier Galletti and Claude Matter, I was immediately struck by the great many samples of building materials adorning the conference room. They use these when they are discussing the various material and constructional aspects of their current, past and future projects.

One might feel that there is nothing extraordinary about this: the preoccupation with construction materials is currently a theme central to architectural thinking, since *"the identity of buildings, and hence that of their architects, is often linked with the architects' ability to discover materials and to suggest inventive ways of constructing with them that speak of texture and perception"*[1].

In the case of Galletti and Matter, however, this preoccupation does not seem to dominate their projects to the exclusion of all else, as their main focus is on the relationship between architecture, landscape and the surrounding region, in a constant quest to forge links between the complementary levels of a project.

The two had already confronted these questions during their studies at the Swiss Federal Institute of Technology in Lausanne, under the guidance of Professor Martin Steinmann and Professor Luigi Snozzi respectively. There they learnt to consider region and city as compulsory points of reference for a project, and to strip architecture to its bare essentials by taking a very rigorous approach to space and construction.

Galletti & Matter have understood this regional and architectural debate and have demonstrated great talent in their response to it, winning many competitions for their work. This has allowed them to realise some extremely ambitious buildings at a very early stage in their careers, such as the school complex in Fully (1991–1995), the Espace Gruyère conference centre in Bulle (1993–1998), the middle school in Collombey-Muraz (1997–1999) and, more recently, the multi-use sports hall in Renens (2000–2002).

In view of what has been said above, it might seem inappropriate to take the theme of "attention to materials" as the main focus of this article. And yet, is the choice of materials (their texture and their colour) not a determining factor in the dialogue between a piece of architecture and its context?

School and gymnasium, Fully

Espace Gruyère, Bulle

Gymnasium and multi-use hall, Renens

Middle school, Collombey

Does the meaning of a building not derive, in part at least, from the fact that the materials create a relationship with the context? And from this perspective, cannot the same material assume different meanings when considered in different contexts?

These questions, pondered in relation to the architecture of Galletti & Matter, cause us to reorient our point of view and to reflect that the two architects' profound knowledge of materials and will to innovate go hand in hand with a marked interest in region and landscape, and that their choice in the matter of materiality does indeed assume several meanings, the principal one of which remains the relationship with context. In an attempt to better define this relationship between materials and context, I shall restrict myself to analysing two of their creations – the dwelling for two families in Lausanne, and the middle school in Collombey-Muraz – which make radical use of two particular materials, reinforced concrete and industrial glass. Two ordinary materials that have featured widely in the construction of modern architecture, although in the context of contemporary architecture their constructional and expressive possibilities have certainly not been exhausted.

Middle school, Collombey

Two family houses, Lausanne

Walls of reinforced concrete for a contextual analogy

A retaining wall of reinforced concrete, slightly curved, leading us up towards the doorways of two houses; a conspicuous wall of reinforced concrete that retains the earth of the garden further up the slope and is adjoined by other walls, also made of reinforced concrete but serving a different purpose: that of containing the domestic spaces of the two abutting houses, set into the slope at right angles to one another. These are one's first impressions of this *opera prima,* born, as is often the case, from a family's commission: the building of a home for two families on a plot of land in Lausanne, a sloping plot punctuated at its apex by a mansion house dating from the 1930s.

The project required much thought as to the positioning of the building within the site, and the enormous potential for view and contemplation. The two houses were therefore positioned together as a single building realised in two separate, adjoining parts and incorporating two major themes: that of the base platform – serving the purpose of retaining the earth and delimiting the original garden to the property – and that of the view towards the lake and the Alps. The architects' choice of material, reinforced concrete, contrives to confirm and materialise these purposes. As the architects maintain, its use is *"not an aim in itself, but rather a means to organise the desired spaces and views. In this case, it was the obvious choice to hold back the earth, but also because of its archaic quality, which marries well with our vision for this type of dwelling as a place where one puts down roots, a place to which one returns continually".*

Two family houses, Lausanne

Reinforced concrete used to characterise a place and to anchor a specific, domestic way of life there: this affirmation, with its Heideggerian echoes, is at some remove from the heroic connotations of a material presented by the historian Sigfried Giedion in his 1928 work *Bauen in Frankreich Eisen Eisenbeton*[2] as one of the principal foundations of the new architecture. A material which, according to the Modernists, has the capacity to take on inventive new forms and to meet the requirements of the emerging ways of life induced by social changes between the wars[3].

Mies van der Rohe, *The Concrete Country House*, 1923

However, in his enthusiasm for this material with its *"artificial chemical composition"*, Giedion failed to draw attention to a paradox: the fact that, during this period in history, reinforced concrete plays only a very small part in the elaboration of a specific aesthetic (brutalism was to come later, in the 1950s), architects seeking rather to achieve an abstract expressive ideal that was clean-cut and consisted of smooth, purified surfaces with no apparent weight. Among the few notable exceptions to this predominant tendency one can cite *The Concrete Country house* designed by Mies van der Rohe in 1923.

Although this project was not realised, some magnificent drawings by Mies have survived, showing stretched facades made of raw concrete, broken up by various openings. Their texture and their resonance in the light are brought out with touches of charcoal. Non-supporting facades surround internal spaces made fluid by the sporadic nature of the enclosing structures, also in reinforced concrete, allowing use to be made of cantilevered slabs, corner windows, and long thin openings at base level.

Mies does not restrict himself to exploiting the spatial, aesthetic and technical potential created by the use of open plan and reinforced concrete. Taking account of the monolithic nature of the material, he works its volume like a sculptor, carving from a compact, homogeneous block, with *"the skin forming both the roof and the walls"*. Thus he echoes Giedion's affirmation that reinforced concrete is a *"composite material"* capable of shaping *"buildings that crystallise into a single rock"*[4], and he establishes a way of working derived from the plastic qualities of reinforced concrete, which he describes in these terms: *"I cut openings in the walls where I needed them, to frame views or to illuminate spaces"*[5]. The materiality of the Lausanne houses is part of this heritage, the concrete serving to unify the separate parts and giving the whole a monolithic appearance broken up only by openings of various shapes (square, long and thin, on the angles) which frame one's gaze in a different way each time. But the elementary and essential use of concrete, although it may have similarities with Miesian architecture, is still very much indebted to the teachings of Snozzi[6], and to the recognition of historical references within the project. From this perspective, the reduction of architectural language – a process which paradoxically attaches great importance to surface and to the way the material is used – has something of the nature of an attempt at creating unity between the new and the old. *"By analogy, the buildings make explicit reference to the construction methods already present on the site"*[7], through a contemporary, abstract expression which thus weaves links with a context in which are intermixed, on the one hand, memory and history (the garden walls and the brickwork of the master house) and on the other hand, the real and the everyday (the view and the landscape framed by the concrete).

As these houses were being built, work was just coming to an end on a school complex in Fully, the pair's first major project and the outcome of a competition won by them in 1991. Here again, the reference is at once both contextual and historical, as witnessed by the dialogue that the building opens up simultaneously with the rock, the vineyards and the existing school. As for the positioning of the building, it was set very precisely on the remains of an old dyke, and the rocks extracted from the dyke were

Luigi Snozzi, Kalman house in Brione s/Minusio, 1976

Two family houses, Lausanne

used in the construction of some of the walls. However, the architects rather left this approach behind them when, some years later, they won the prize for the Collombey-Muraz middle school, a simple, compact construction that gave them the opportunity to experiment with a different material: industrial glass.

Walls of glass for an imaginary context

At first sight, one's main impression of this middle school is of walls of translucent Profilit glass, oriented along the line of the Rhône Valley; two walls of glass rising three storeys high, which constitute the two main facades of the school and which *"filter the light of the Valais across their entire surface"*[8]; whole glazed surfaces, "dotted" with windows that seem at first to be arranged in a random fashion; glazed facades that underline the presence of the wooded hills in the surrounding landscape by their brightness and their lustre.

At Collombey-Muraz, the glass takes on an imposing power and almost solid physical presence quite at variance with the qualities of lightness and transparency that make it, along with reinforced concrete, one of the construction materials most representative of modernity. One example of this modernity which remains an icon is the Glass Pavilion realised by German architect Bruno Taut for the Cologne Werkbund Exhibition in 1914, an edifice celebrated in the prose poem *Glasarchitektur* by Paul Scheerbart, published the same year. But it would be wrong to maintain that the essential good fortune of this material is limited strictly to its qualities of transparency. In his poem, Scheerbart (who also considers reinforced concrete to be an ideal material, although unfortunately not very aesthetic) advocates *"the adoption of a glass architecture which lets the light of the sun and the brightness of the moon and the stars into dwelling places, not just through a few windows but also through the greatest possible number of walls – walls made entirely of glass (...)"*[9]. Thus he makes a clear distinction between openings fitted with panes of transparent glass, intended essentially to allow one to look through them, and double walls of translucent glass which he would like to see used to form the outer shell of buildings, with the main purpose of filtering the light.

Scheerbart desires to control the intensity of the light; he aspires to muffled, introverted ambiences, bathed in changing light filtered through glass screens. In fact his intention is *"not to obtain a perfect outlook, but rather to educate people as to how to receive light, how to diffuse it and distribute it generously"*. He seeks to bring out *"a new kind of photosensitivity, an ability to take in and make best use of the phenomenon of light that would become an ability and a skill possessed by all, a source of acute and subtle physical and moral pleasure for everyone (...)"*[10]. Pleasure also engendered by the effects of artificial lighting, gene-rated by electric lamps arranged between the walls or inside the rooms. Twinkling light that *"will make the whole glass house into one great lantern, blazing in the night through summer and winter like fireflies and glow-worms"*[11].

This last quotation, taken from *Glasarchitektur*, could be illustrated to striking effect by images of the Collombey school at night: the glass walls of the two main facades lit up like a great lantern, a vast light source in the darkness of the plain. In this building, Galletti & Matter play with the two different properties of glass: its transparency and its translucency. Thus they make a clear distinction between the vertical openings, through which one gazes out, and the expanses of the glass walls composed of vertical panes of Profilit attached to aluminium cross-beams, which on the contrary contain one's gaze.

Bruno Taut, *Alpine Architecture*, 1919

Gymnasium and multi-use hall, Renens

Middle school, Collombey

Glasshouses

The relationship with the site is present right from conception. The form of the building, its orientation, corresponds to the rough outlines of the landscape, consisting of the horizontals of the Rhône plain and the mountains. This relationship is reinforced by the arrangement of viewing points, strictly controlled and differentiated by the shape of the openings: vertical windows, at different heights, in the classrooms, like paintings reflecting the contrasting shades of the vegetation on the hills; horizontal slits on the landings to give a better idea of the breadth of the valley; and lastly, random openings positioned to frame the view of the solid mountains in a picturesque and striking way.

But through the medium of the glass and through its use, the architects set this direct relationship aside to introduce another level of discourse: now it is the glasshouses dotted about the plain and illuminating it at night that serve as a model, the qualities of the ephemeral being transposed into buildings that are institutional and, by definition, durable. Thus the use of glass harks back to a context which is at once real – the glasshouses are indeed present in the Rhône Valley – and also imaginary, since they correspond to this general *"mythical background"* against *"which the architects delineate their work"*[12]; as it happens, the plain in its original state, serving its agricultural and horticultural vocation, to which the architects make reference by their use of glass.

Gymnasium and multi-use hall,
Renens

Middle school, Collombey

Prefabricated elements,
Collège de la Carrière, Crissier

Textures: working to the limits

Concrete, used to root a domestic way of life in a place laden with history; glass to create analogies with utilitarian buildings: in both cases, the material is used to exalt the viewpoints, to manage the supply of light and, at the same time, to give the building a meaning that is in keeping with the context into which it is placed.

After Collombey-Muraz, others of the pair's more recent projects have reintroduced the same dissociations of the outlook and the light, the window and the expanse of glass. In the gymnastics hall at Renens (2000–2002), the openings in the concrete plinth are cut out apparently at random, while the main light, lateral and zenithal, is diffused by an enclosing structure of Profilit covered in polycarbonate. The principle here is that of dissociation of the outlook and the light, governed by complementary materials. In other projects – the multi-use hall and library in Collombey (2001–2004), the Collège de la Carrière in Crissier (2003, still under construction) – the concrete is prefabricated, adding a touch of pragmatism to a discourse on materials that becomes increasingly complex in its quest for other meanings.

Among this diversity, however, one again finds the same interest in materials – not in a constructional sense, concerned with their structural potential, but in the sense of the constitution of a surface, a texture. This is working on the limits, on those enclosing structures, the expressive force and the ability of which to arouse emotions depend upon the spirit of the materials, which in turn seems to reflect another spirit: that of the places that Galletti & Matter hold in such affection.

1 M. C. Loriers, "Matériauphilie",
   Techniques & architecture, no. 472,
   2004, p. 77.
2 S. Giedion, *Building in France, Building in
   Iron, Building in Ferro concrete* (1928),
   Oxford University Press, New York, 1995.
3 See also on this subject C. Simonnet,
   L'architecture ou la fiction constructive,
   Les Editions de la Passion, Paris, 2001,
   pp. 22-35.
4 S. Giedion, *Building in France, Building in
   Iron, Building in Ferro concrete* (1928),
   Oxford University Press, New York, 1995,
   p. 66.
5 Mies van der Rohe, "Bauen", G, no. 2,
   1923, p. 1.
6 E. Lapierre, with C. Chevrier, E. Pinard,
   P. Salerno, "Entretien avec Aurelio
   Galfetti, Luigi Snozzi et Livio Vacchini
   sur le béton en tant que matériau de
   construction et mode d'expression",
   archithese, no. 2, 1986, pp. 11–14 and 32.
7 I. Lamunière, P. Devanthéry, "Tout bois,
   tout béton, oui mais... Deux réalisations de
   Brauen & Waechli et Galletti & Matter".
   Faces, no. 25, 1991, p. 37.
8 G. D., "Olivier Galletti et Claude Matter.
   Ecole secondaire Collombey, Suisse",
   amc, no. 105, 2000, p. 42.
9 P. Scheerbart, *L'Architecture de verre*
   (1914), Circé, Strasbourg, 1995, p. 29.
10 D. Payot, "La société barbare de Paul
   Scheerbart" in P. Scheerbart,
   L'Architecture de verre, op. cit., pp. 12-13.
11 P. Scheerbart, *L'Architecture de verre*,
   p. 64.
12 E. Lapierre, with C. Chevrier, E. Pinard,
   P. Salerno, *Architecture du réel, architecture contemporaine en France*,
   Editions du Moniteur, Paris, 2003, p. 33.

Galletti & Matter: a serene architecture

Pierre-Alain Croset

I first met Olivier Galletti and Claude Matter in 1987, in Luigi Snozzi's design studio at the Swiss Federal Institute of Technology in Lausanne. They were bright students,

Town hall, Monthey

belonging to a very talented generation; yet there was nothing about them to suggest that soon they would have won several major competitions and begun to create a body of work that would achieve great significance within only 15 years: 21 buildings realized out of a total of nearly 100 projects. Compared to others of Snozzi's most outstanding pupils, they seemed to be almost "withdrawn": in fact their reserve, their discretion and even their politeness hid qualities of rigour and simplicity that were very soon to become the principal qualities of their architecture. It was thanks to these qualities that an international jury – which included Àlvaro Siza and Aurelio Galfetti – awarded them first prize in the competition to design a town hall for Monthey (1989). This major success, coming shortly before they graduated, provided them with the necessary basis upon which to open their own practice, without actually guaranteeing that the project would be realised. Following this dazzling start, I had the opportunity to meet them again as a member of the competition juries at Martigny (1989) and at Monthey (1990, 1991). Later I discovered through various publications that, despite their youth, their work possessed a solidity and maturity that quickly won much admiration in international architectural circles. Firstly, their dwelling for

Andrea Palladio Prize

AV Monografias

two families in Lausanne, designed in 1987 and built in 1992, was selected in 1993 for its obvious topographical and tectonic qualities as one of the 20 finalists for the prestigious Andrea Palladio architectural prize, an award specially for architects under 40 years of age and boasting a particularly eminent jury (Francesco Dal Co, Rafael Moneo, Manfredo Tafuri). Secondly, a monograph about the Collombey-Muraz middle school was published in a special issue of *AV Monografias*, devoted to Swiss architecture (no. 89, May/June 2001, "Materia Suiza"). The editors of the journal took the opportunity to use a close-up photo of the building's glass facade to create a curious photomontage representing a kind of visual summary of the issue's contents: against the apparently neutral background of the Profilit panes, the windows are shown as framing not panes of glass, but samples of materials characterising the facades of some of the buildings most representative of the latest trends in Swiss architecture. Thus one recognises for example the Vaduz museum (Kerez, Morger & Degelo), the Swiss Embassy in Berlin (Diener & Diener), the St. Jakob stadium in Basel (Herzog & de Meuron) and the Vrin abattoir (Caminada).

However, this fragment of "typically Swiss" facade is not in any way representative of the work of Galletti and Matter.

Their architecture in fact expresses its major qualities in its relationship with the urban and geographical context, and consequently cannot be confined to an image of the object taken in isolation. Thus it resists the excesses of a certain manneristic tendency in most recent Swiss architecture to express itself in a fetishistic love of materials and in a kind of falling back on questions of pure constructional aesthetics. This tendency seems to favour the rhetorical figure of synecdoche – the part to represent the whole, the material to represent the object – to the detriment of the quality of relationship between form and function that has traditionally characterised the ethics of modernist architectural design. The fact that the issue of *Arquitectura Viva* is

"

structured according to a categorisation of objects by material –
concrete, wood, glass, metal – seems to tie in with this reductionist
tendency. To Galletti and Matter, however, the choice of a material
is not an end in itself. Concrete, wood, glass and metal have all
been used in turn to suit different briefs and to dialogue with
diverse contexts; this demonstrates an open, anti-ideological and
even pragmatic attitude towards the question of the materialisation
of a project. Concrete – a hommage to their master Luigi Snozzi
– thus characterises the dwelling for two families in Lausanne, giving substance to the idea of building the base platform for the
master house. Wood is an integral part of the context of the

Two family houses, Lausanne

Espace Gruyère fair and conference centre in Bulle – a physical presence in the
neighbouring sawmill, a natural presence in the landscape that forms a backdrop to
the town – and thus it plays a part in connoting the rural character of this "cathe-
dral for cows". The glass used in the Collombey school, and the metallic outer shell
enveloping the spaces of the gymnastics hall, imply a more abstract relationship with
the geographical context: placed in the open countryside of the Rhône Valley, the
expanse of glass and the perforated sheet metal lose any local connotation and
become a statement of universalist modernity.

Espace Gruyère, Bulle

The happiness of children

Like all good architecture, the buildings of Galletti and Matter resist the immediate
seduction of photographs and reveal their most secret qualities only when one actually visits them. The materials mentioned above involve different registers of perception: some years on, it is possible to remember concrete for its roughness, wood
for its smell, glass for its luminosity. What memories will be retained by the children
who fill Galletti and Matter's schools? Of the middle school in Collombey, memories
will no doubt remain of the particularly brightly lit classrooms, the framed views out
over the plain and the mountains, the generous expanses of the corridors. The children
at the Fully primary school, on the other hand, will remember the happiness of break
times spent playing on the steps of the covered playground, in the shade of the soar-
ing rock; and of running between the sculptural lanterns that occupy the schoolyard.

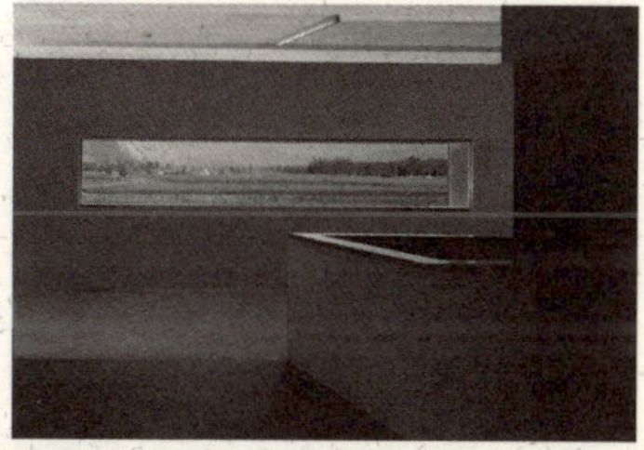

Middle school, Collombey

At the Saillon primary school, their finest memories will be of the central space
of the schoolyard, and in particular of the great wooden canopy from which
one can admire the view of the old village.

The schools of Galletti and Matter have not forgotten the great functional-
ist lessons of Duiker, Beaudouin and Lods, Terragni or Neutra: "air and sun"
penetrate from all sides, while great attention is however paid to what is
today a major concern, the energy costs, in response to the very strict
demands of the Swiss standards. The Collombey facade is the most successful
in this respect, and since its construction Galletti and Matter have continued
to experiment with innovative constructional solutions dictated by the ethics
of sustainable development.

When one visits these schools, however, what strikes one the most is the particular way that they not only enhance these quite exceptional geographical
sites, but also integrate fragments of existing architecture and improve
them by creating a new context around them. In Saxé, the new building con-

School and Gymnasium,
Fully

Primary school extension,
Saillon

trives by its extremely precise positioning to enhance the old school at the border of
the village; but most importantly, the excavation work and backfilling skilfully change the
topography in such a way as to create a new relationship between the rock, the
school and the rich sequence of the external spaces. In Saillon, the brief of creating

Primary school extension, Saillon

Library patio, Collombey

View from the swimming pool to the patio, Collombey

a modest extension (comprising only four classrooms) is brilliantly interpreted as an opportunity to redefine the pre-existing school complex: on the one hand, by giving it a new facade of a more urban character, defined by a stone "brise-soleil" that carries on a dialogue with the stone houses of the old bourg in the distance. On the other hand, despite the limitations of a meagre budget, the architects succeed in enhancing the internal schoolyard by making it a place that brings together the different elements of the old part and the extension, where previously all dialogue between the architecture and the context was lacking. In Collombey, the new middle school building redefines the relationships between the different parts of the pre-existing school complex: the covered porch, looking like a great table placed between the new wing and the old buildings, forms a new entranceway along the length of the football pitch that gives structure to the urban composition of the various minimalist "boxes". Two years after the completion of the new wing, Galletti and Matter won the competition to create new infrastructures for the school in 2001. This gave them the opportunity to integrate the new library and a second gymnasium in a very skilful way that ultimately reinforces the urban function of the covered porch. Thus the quality of the intervention can be gauged by the architects' ability to create meaningful relationships between new and existing parts. On a visit to the school complex one comes across several places that take one completely by surprise, such as the small patio area created between the existing swimming pool and the new library: a real secret garden, containing two fine trees, onto which the fullheight sliding glass doors of the library can be opened wide. The patio catches a very attractive light, filtered through the vegetation, which enhances the internal spaces of the swimming pool and the library.

Creating intermediate spaces between town and country

On several occasions, Galletti and Matter have demonstrated great skill in the way they have enhanced some magnificent sites: the precise framing of the views of the landscape, the discretion and simplicity of the new spaces, the precision of the positioning. These are all characteristics of the Saxe and Collombey schools, and also the dwelling for two families in Lausanne, so that the new architecture establishes a relationship of appropriateness with the landscape. The Collège de la Carrière in Crissier, currently nearing completion, confirms the topographical sensitivity of the architects, who exploit the possibilities of a sloping plot to best effect. On the one hand, the positioning of the gymnasium and the wing of classrooms at the base of the slope reduces the visual impact of the school on the landscape; on the other hand, the great lime tree that already existed on the site is not only preserved, but made the founding newel of the design, with a square built around it to give access to the library pavilion. This square, delimited by a portico that opens onto a large belevedere terrace above the wing of classrooms, has a character all of its own, neither truly urban nor truly rural: it is a public space of a new kind, a perfect solution to the need to create places for socialisation in the residential areas that are gradually taking over the fallow farmland around urban conglomerations. Galletti and Matter make intelligent use of the fact that it is possible to build schools in Switzerland without perimeter fences: they exploit this to create a great freedom to wander round the building, and in the case of the school in Crissier they

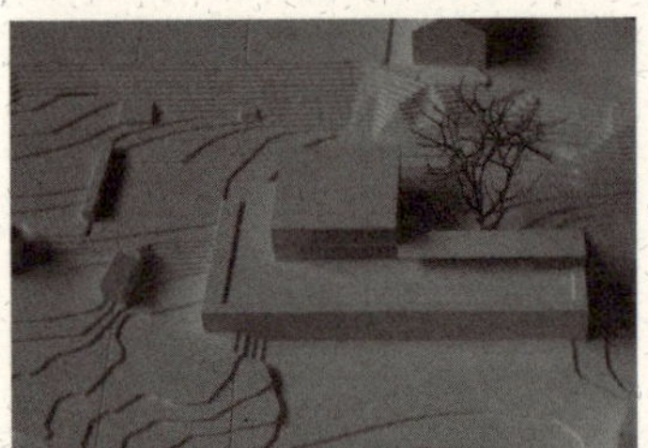

Collège de la Carrière, Crissier

make best use of a public footpath that crosses the site. This same principle of freedom to wander round a public building characterises their interesting design for a village hall in Ballaigues, set in an orchard on a slope. The orchard becomes the urban space connecting the car park at the top of the slope, the terrace outside the foyer of the multi-use hall halfway down and the new square at the bottom. The architectural, or even sculptural treatment of the volumes is also significant: the large sheet metal roof that envelopes the whole building dialogues with the traditional village roofs, yet at the same time asserts a discreet monumentality that connotes the public dimension of the architecture.

Galletti and Matter are interested in reinterpreting certain typical elements of tra-ditional rural architecture in a resolutely contemporary architectural language. However, they do not apply this interest only in a rural context. In Renens, in a peripheral urban site marked by the presence of a park with large trees, the two volumes of the gymnastics hall and the multi-use hall of Les Pepinières are designed as two elementary "boxes", shrouded in a skin of glass and metal, which take their inspiration from the architecture of rural barns to create a vast intermediate space beneath the roof, significantly reducing the building's energy costs. As in the projects analysed above, the positioning of the two "boxes" in the site takes skilled advantage of the slope to make best use of the pre-existing park as a space connecting the different entrances of the gymnastics hall in the lower part of the park and the multi-use hall in the upper part.

Gymnasium and multi-use hall, Ballaigues

Thus rural architecture is used not as a formal reference in the work of Galletti and Matter, but rather as an ethical model for a "way of building" inspired by the principles of economy, simplicity and respect for the site. The architects' ability to use the technical innovations in contemporary architecture to best effect is thus made to serve their conviction that the architect's profession involves a precise social responsibility: that of constructing reference places for the public life – schools, town halls, village halls, covered markets – while striving to enhance the natural and the built-up landscape, and at the same time to respect the new conditions of sustainable development.

Gymnasium and multi-use hall, Renens

Strategy and planning/ pragmatism and imagination

Olivier Galletti – Claude Matter

This inventory gives us an opportunity to pause, to look back over the works we have accomplished. At first sight, the various projects described may seem fundamentally different to one another. The theme that they clearly all share is the continual quest to create buildings that bring out the intrinsic qualities of each location. In each of the projects, this fundamental quality is the fruit of our first thoughts, our initial conceptual choices.

After our studies, when our first project was built, we found out how difficult it is to give life to these initial ideas. Although we thought that we could rely on these premises as the basis for a series of decisions that would give substance to the future building. We understand that these concepts remain abstract without wishing to discover all they hold. At the centre of the study therefore it is an approach which starts by listening and understanding a process of abstraction capable of revealing the properties of a place, a function and a building.

At this stage the project takes on a life of its own as one steps back to let the hidden energies of the initial sketches come forth.

Developing a project is to us the equivalent of diving into the instant of "doing", of allowing oneself to be guided by the will, the breath of the project, by its inevitable contradictions, without wishing to surmount them in a perfectly unitary whole.

In a section of "La Promesse" speaking of detective stories, Dürrenmatt offered us a clearer understanding of this attitude patiently applied:

"You don't try to grapple with a reality that keeps eluding us, you just set up a manageable world. That world may be perfect, but it's a lie. Forget about perfection if you want to make headway and get at the way things actually are, at reality, like a man; otherwise you'll be left fiddling around with useless stylistic exercises. (...) I know very well what a dubious bunch we all are, how little we can accomplish, how easily we make mistakes; but I also know that we have to act anyway, even at the risk of acting wrongly." [1]

So our way of tackling the project remains open-minded. The initial abstraction of the concept does not seek to resolve all the problems; it gradually allows itself to be contaminated, enriched by the many unknown quantities inherent to any construction. At each stage of the project, some of the problems are knowingly left unsolved; their resolution is kept for a later stage, a different approach.

For example, in the school project in Collombey, the initial idea of a vertical framing of the views in the east and west facades became richer to take account of the architectural and technical problems. The search for solutions which aim to solve technical problems such as integrations of solar protection, natural ventilation via windows which open or the integration of translucid insulation up to a maximum height of 2m in profilit glass modules, opened up a direction which offered a solution to the architectural problem of plastic discontinuity of translucid elements which was posed by the initial idea of a floor to ceiling window. The new solution integrating shorter windows reinforces the plastic unity of the envelope and creates the language of the building. Thus the work is not confined to the single vision of the initial concept. It has fed on the history of the project, the possibilities connected with the different ways of realising it. In an age where craftmanship is no longer the reality of the building site, the project takes shape on the basis of the installation of numerous prefabricated elements. Borrowing,

Middle school, Collombey, construction and model

moving, assembling and diverting fragments of technologies that are often heterogeneous, the architect's constructive invention then no longer follows the same process as the engineer.

It flourishes along a path that approaches that of the "Bricoleur" by Lévi-Strauss in the quest for a dialogue with the project:

"...The poetry of the 'bricolage' also derives above all from the fact that it does not limit itself to accomplishing or executing; it 'speaks', not only to objects, as we have already shown, but also through objects: telling us, through the choices that it makes between limited possibilities, about the character and the life of its author."[2]

Middle school, Collombey, construction and model

1   Friedrich Dürrenmatt, "The Pledge", Penguin, 2000, p. 9.
2   Claude Lévi-Strauss, "The Savage Mind", Weidenfeld and Nicholson, 1974, p. 35.

The site was already built up with a primary school, a gymnastics hall, a swimming pool and a day nursery.

The project reorganises the whole school complex on either side of a covered schoolyard. This constitutes a central backbone to which all the elements of the complex are grafted. The middle school building is positioned at right angles to the covered yard, along the line of the valley, enhancing the fundamental characteristics of the site:

- The vertical windows facing the slopes accentuate the features of the Valais landscape in succession: the plain, the mountain, the sky.

- The long windows facing the valley accentuate the specific nature of a glacial valley: its width, the horizontality of the ground, the power of the mountains bordering it.

- The vertical windows of the east and west facades are integrated into a system of Profilit glazing with integral translucent insulation. This type of glazing filters direct sunlight and gives

a gentle, even light at all times. The sun protections are provided only to prevent the building from overheating in the summer period; the rest of the year the sunshine provides thermic gains. This solution offers optimal lighting of the buildings with a central corridor typology and ensures excellent energy efficiency.

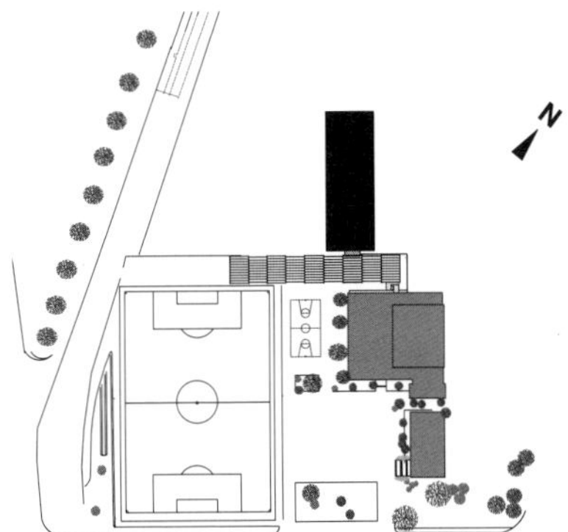

Site plan

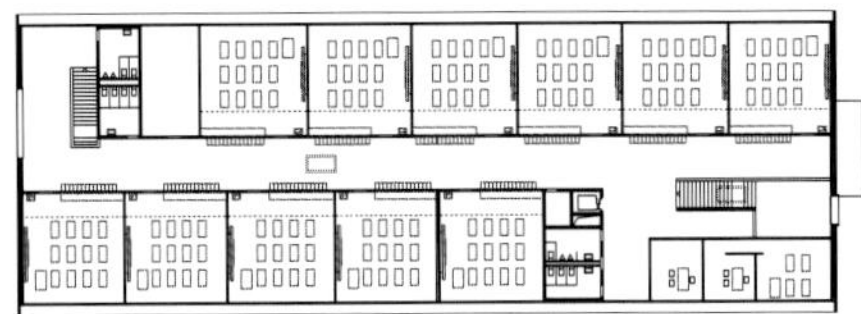

Second floor level

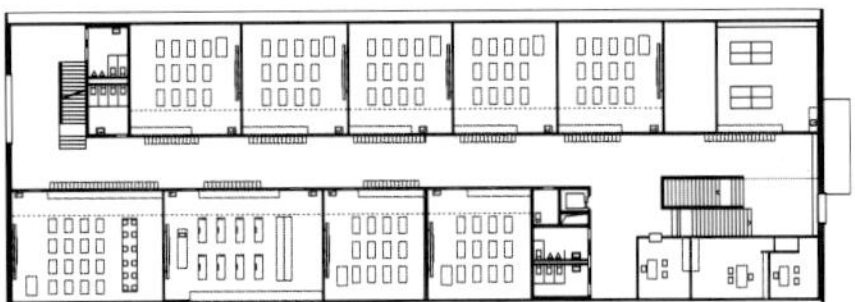

First floor level

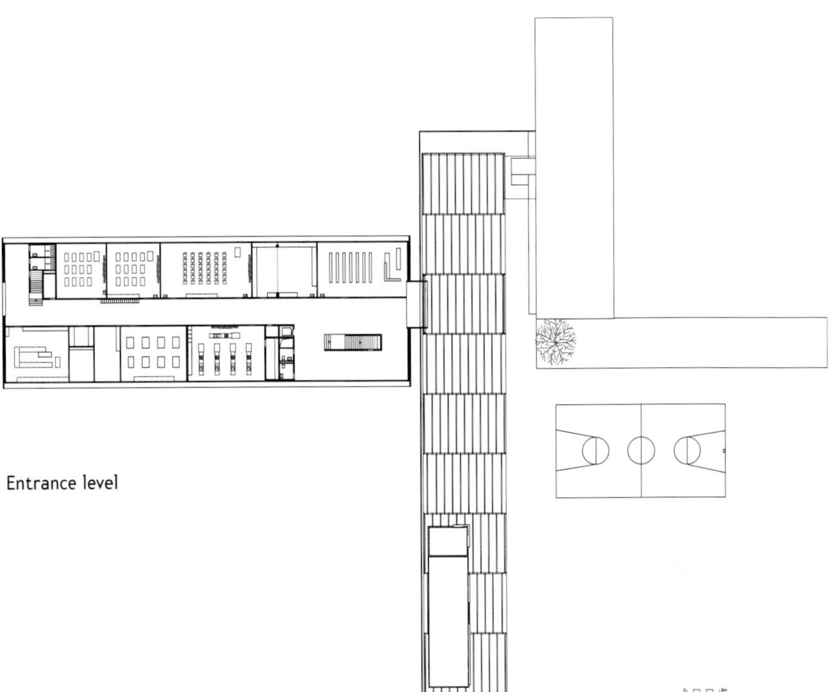

Entrance level

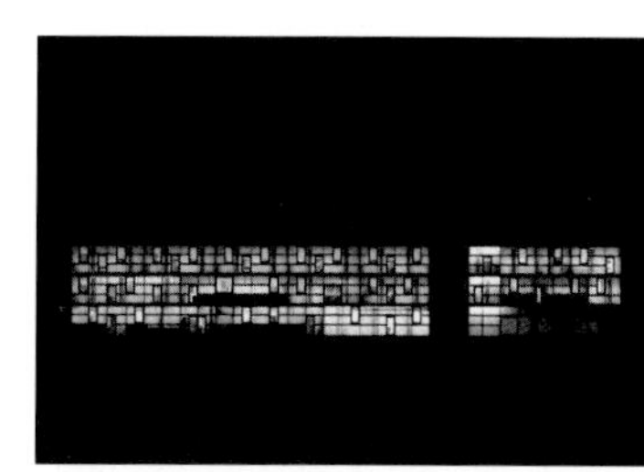

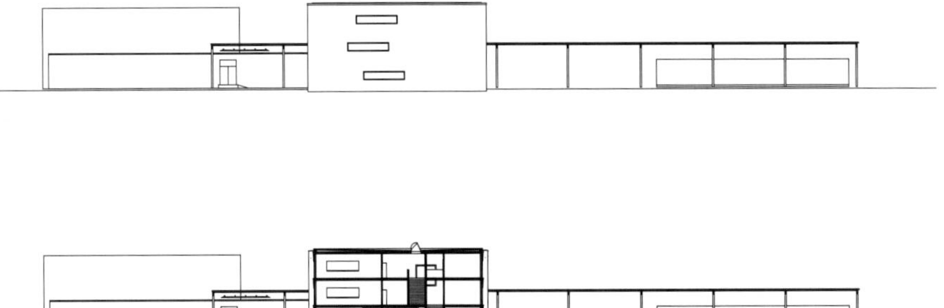

North facade and cross section

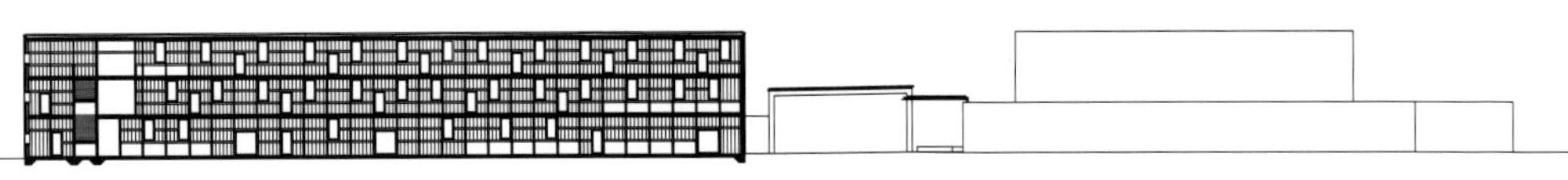

Long section through corridor

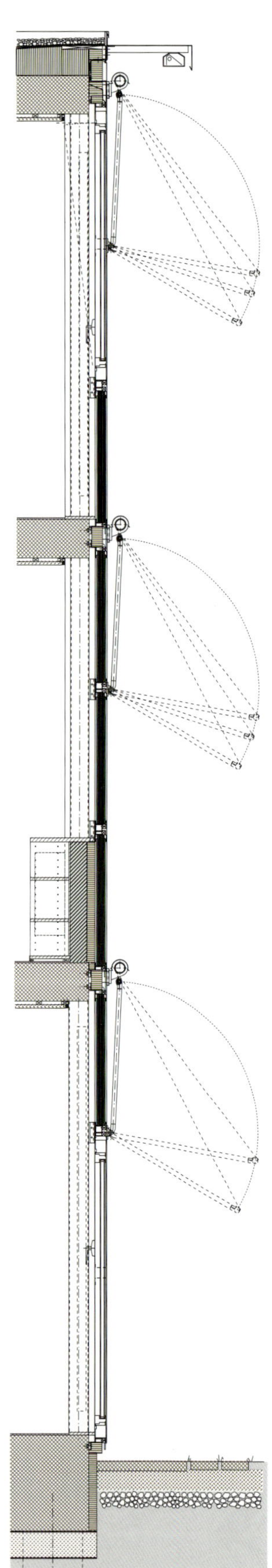

Facade sectional detail

In this location characterised by the presence of the historic market town, and given an existing building of complex geometry, the modesty of the building brief does not permit a complete reorganisation of the existing building.

However, given a building that is arranged around a central space while turning its back on it, the project proposes to complement it by constructing a central schoolyard capable of becoming the heart of the school.

This site welcomes the new covered schoolyard, the larch ceiling and floor of which make reference to the architecture of the medieval market town. In a similar way the stone facade forming a sunshade over the classrooms opens up a dialogue with this mineral architecture.

Implantation concept

Bird's-eye view of the previous situation

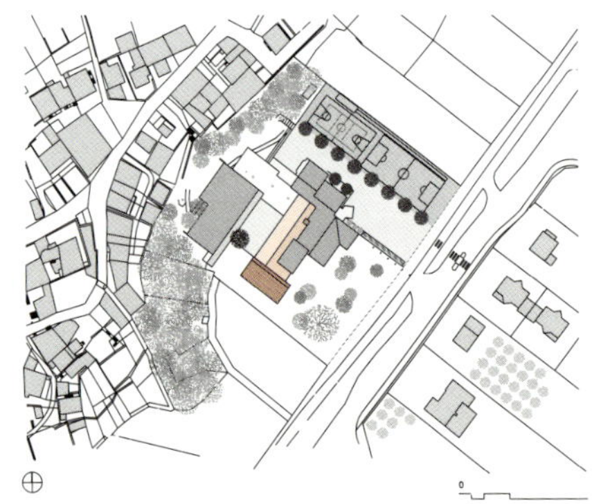

Site plan

Long section

Cross section

First floor plan

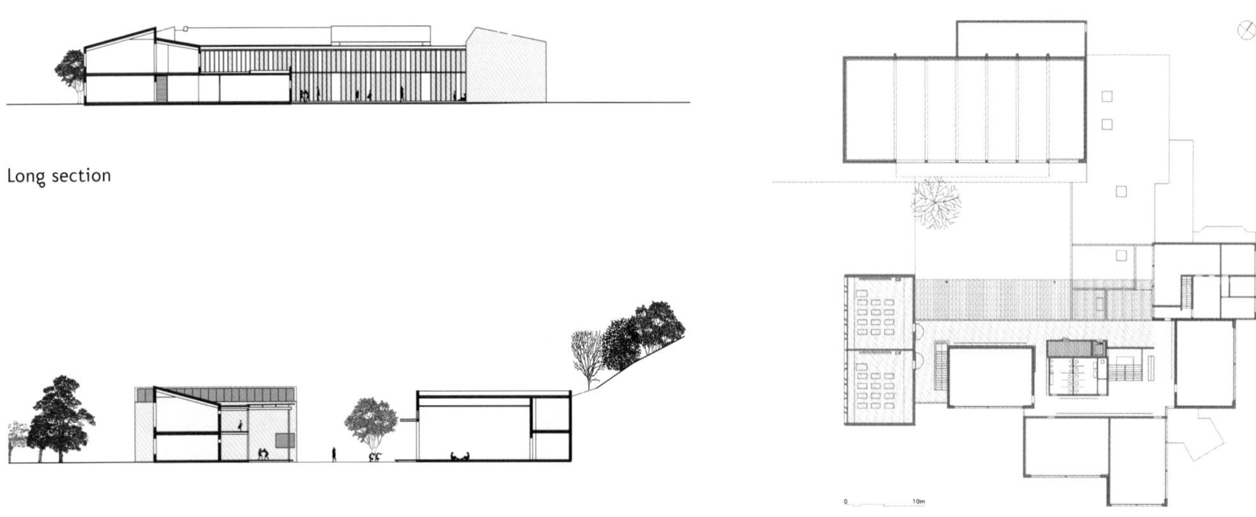

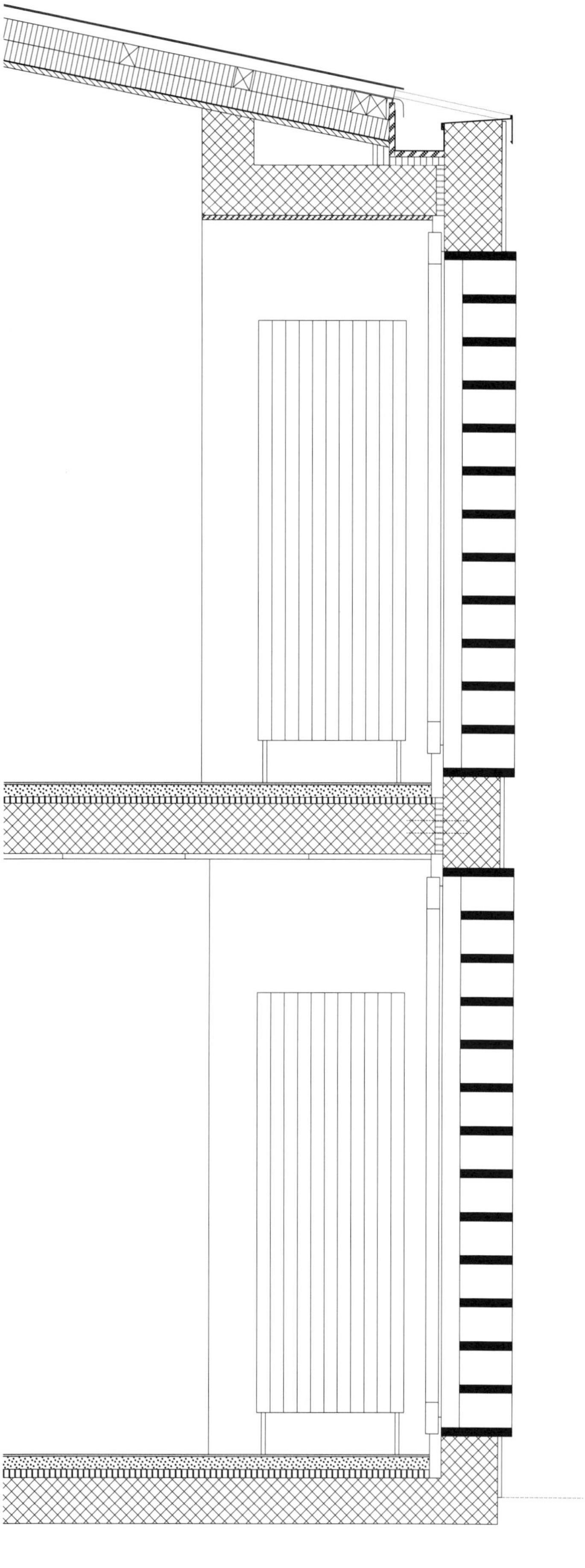

South-west facade sectional detail

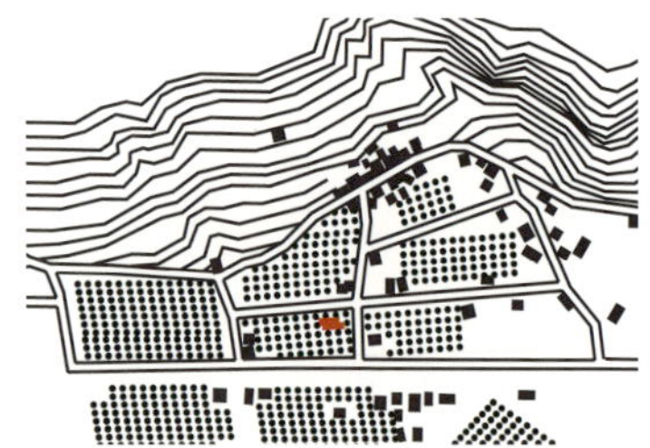

Site plan

Situation concept

Located in the Rhône plain at the foot of the Chavalard, in an area of the town without interest. The plan is based on the organisation of the orchard and on the strong presence of the mountain slope. The building takes the form of two strips that echo the geometry and volumetry of the orchard.

To the south, the volume of the bed-rooms remains in close relationship with the crowns of the pear trees.

To the north, the volume of the living room rises above the orchard to offer a view of the mountainside and the peaks.

Views concept

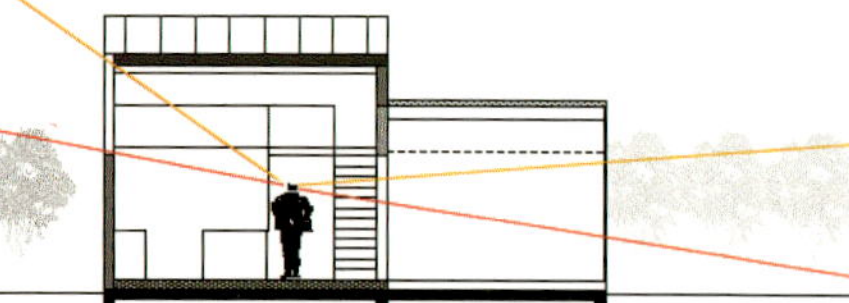

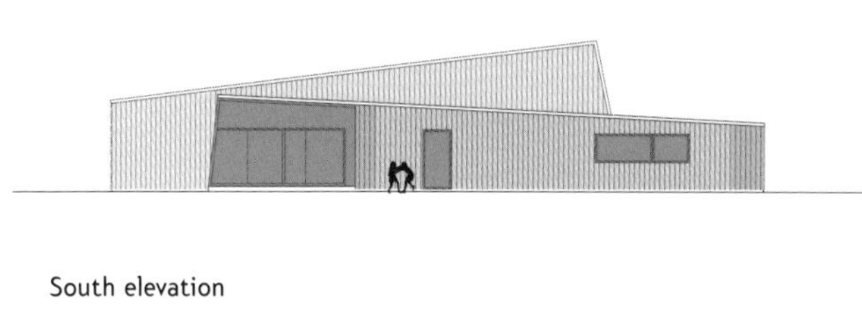

South elevation

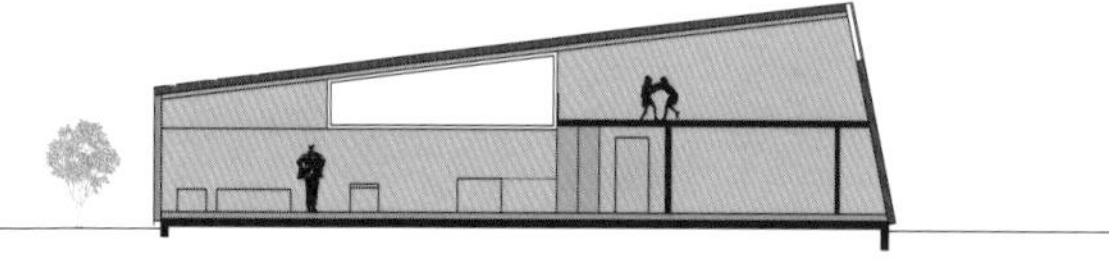

Long section

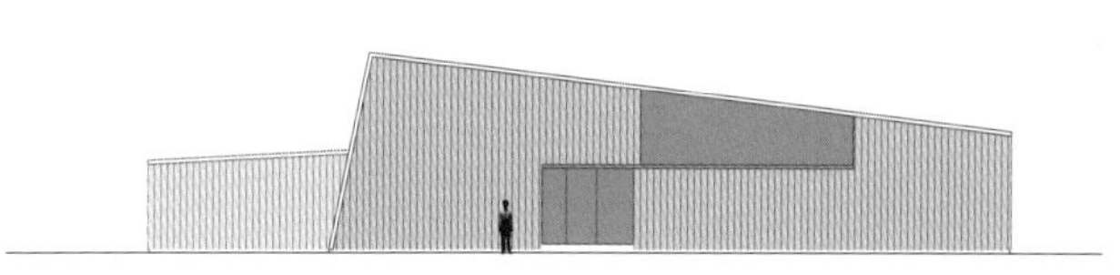

North elevation with entrance

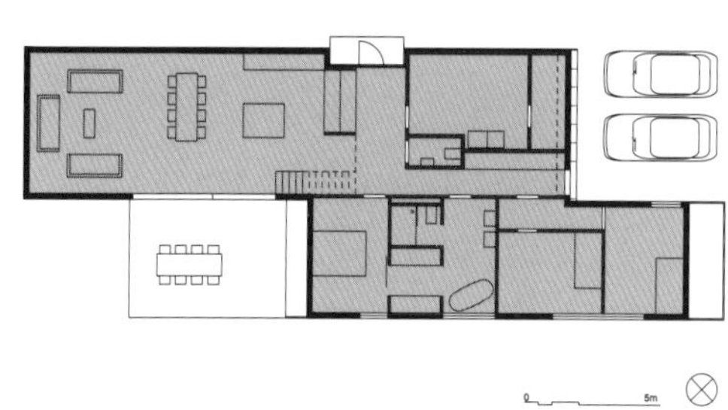

Entrance level

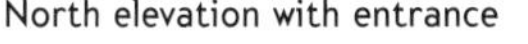

Today's social practices are part of a double reality: the one physical, the other a media reality. This has modified our relationship with our home world.

The housing proposed is arranged around a central foyer structured by the light into two spaces, the one introverted, the other extraverted.

The first space is extraverted because it is a thoroughfare; its external continuation opens it up into its immediate environment. Here you are exposed to the variations of the seasons, the weather and the hours of the day.
The second space, set further back, is introverted. With its indirect lighting it is intended for TV or the computer or their future incarnations. In this alcove, the artificial climate of electronic media reigns.

Apart from the bedrooms at the front, the living space stretches between two focal points: the fireplace and the screen.

Increasingly, habitat will be required to satisfy heterogeneous needs. The fusion of people's private and professional spheres, the coexistence of several generations and the disappearance of the predominant family model make the task of planning for these needs less certain.

A typology characterised by two valencies and two rooms with separate access allows itself to be adapted to suit the fluctuations in people's way of living.

This guarantees, on the one hand, simultaneous multiple usage (office, separate bedroom, working from home) and on the other hand, great flexibility over time (studio and two, three, four, five, six or even seven half-rooms). This spatial and functional flexibility is synonymous with economy of means; one and the same structure fulfils all the complex requirements of an open brief.

A semi-private external space, the landing, replaces the traditional circulation areas.

Entrance

The living room

On the edge

	Project	Realisation
Espace Gruyère, ice rink and exhibition centre, **Bulle**	1993	1998
Dwelling for a family, **Lausanne**	1996	
Multi-use hall, **Grône**	1999	
Gymnasium and multi-use hall, **Renens**	2000	2002
Phoniatrics and logopedics unit, Chuv, **Lausanne**	2000	2004
Multi-use hall and library, **Collombey**	2001	2003
Concert hall and casino, **Sion**	2001	

Place des Albergeux

Previous building before demolition

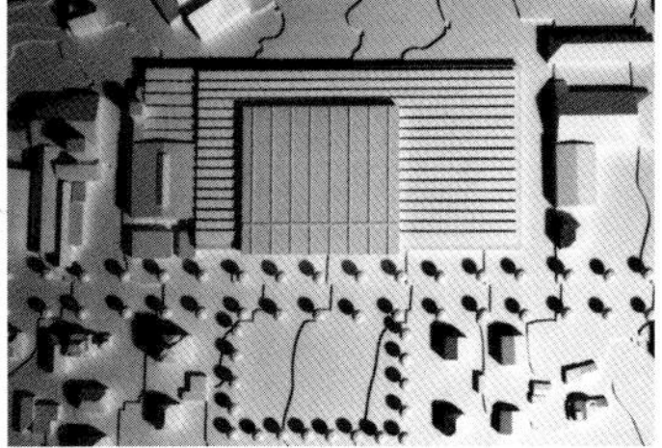

The brief for the new covered market in Bulle is very unusual: the principal aim of the building is to accommodate up to 500 cows or bulls when the main cattle markets are held. However, the building also accommodates an ice rink and various trade fairs and exhibitions.

Construction of a building of this size (120 m x 70 m at ground level) obliged us to consider three questions:
- The building's relationship with the urban structure.
- Its ability to meet the brief's demand for flexibility.
- The solution that should be chosen to cover this vast space: the roofing.

The covered market acts as an interface between region, town and district. It is composed of two volumes that interpenetrate one another. The wooden one holds the exhibition hall; it ensures the continuation of the existing built structure by its horizontality. The other, in copper, houses the theatre, ice rink and service building; it signals the covered market and becomes its entrance. By its position, this volume reconstructs the north face of the place des Albergeux and creates a relationship with the village.

The introverted, horizontal space of the exhibition hall is defined by a wooden enclosure in keeping with the rural atmosphere dictated by the brief. Its roof of cattle sheds provides the natural light and ventilation needed by the animals.

The roof is planned as a succession of pens made of squared-off timbers, 90 cms apart, supported on a steel structure. The light is thus reflected and filtered by the structure, forming a kind of luminous wooden ceiling.

The theatre with its covering of practical laminated wood reflects the light and defines the ambience of this space. The interior walls of the hall are designed to offer good acoustics: perforated panelling, roof of wood fibre bonded with cement, terraces of nailed planks.

The main elements creating the image and the ambience of the building are made of wood: the facade and roof of the exhibition hall, the facade and structure of the ice rink/theatre.

The covering over the facade of the exhibition space is made of several vertical bands of shiplap planks of rough-sawn larch. This appropriation of a common detail of rural architecture forms the continuity of the covering. The alternating of the direction in which the planks overlap plays with the light to make these vast, shaded spaces resonate. The height of the strips (150 cm) is defined so as to utilise the full width of the planks (optimisation of the cutting up of the trunks).

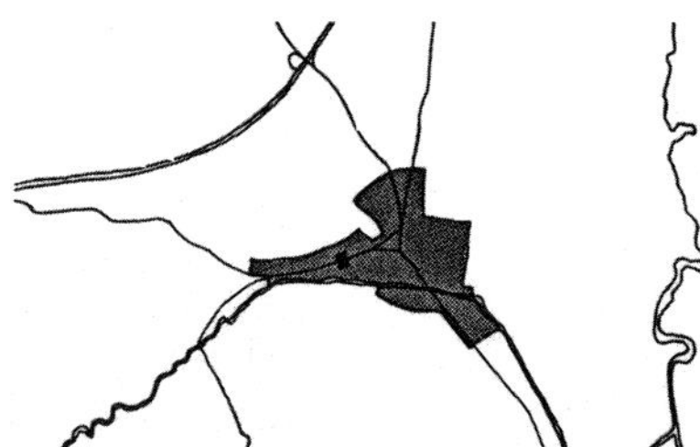

Site plan

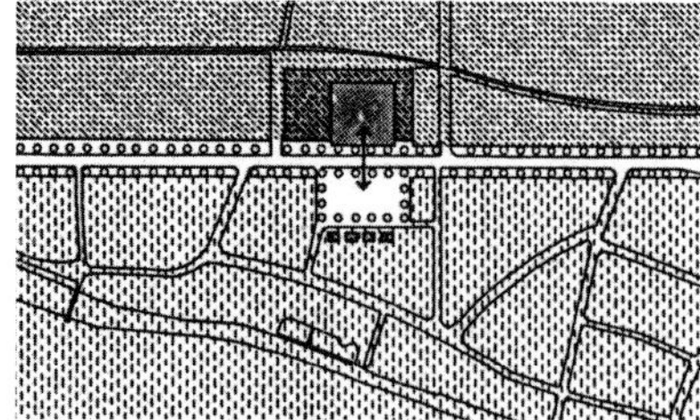

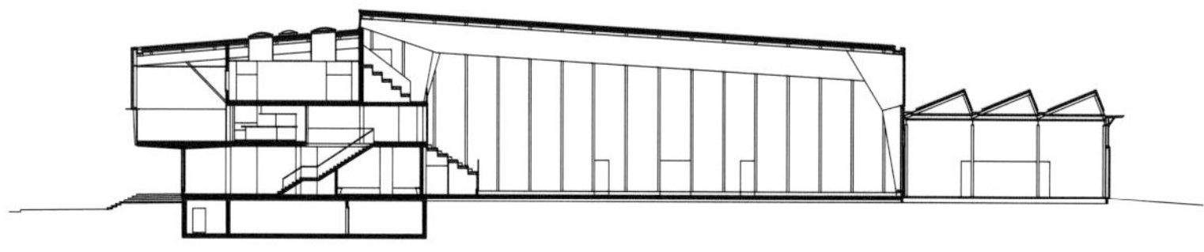

Cross section through presentation hall

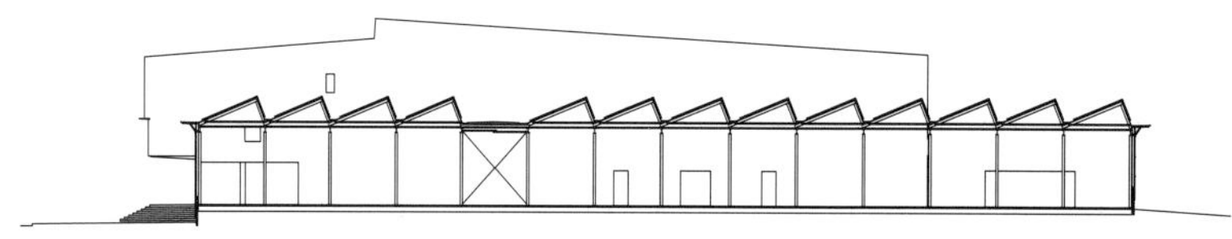

Cross section, sheds

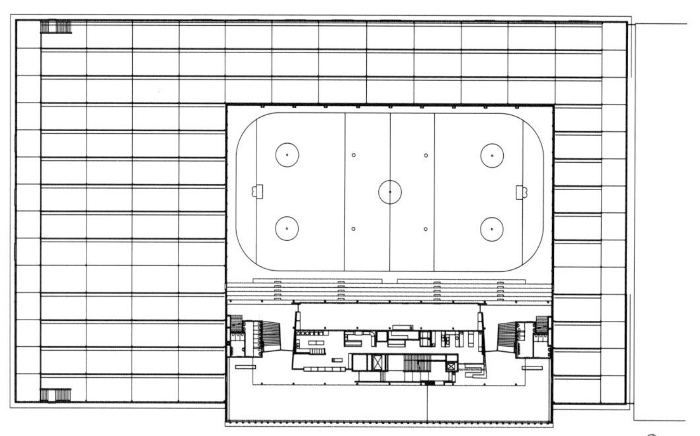

Restaurant level

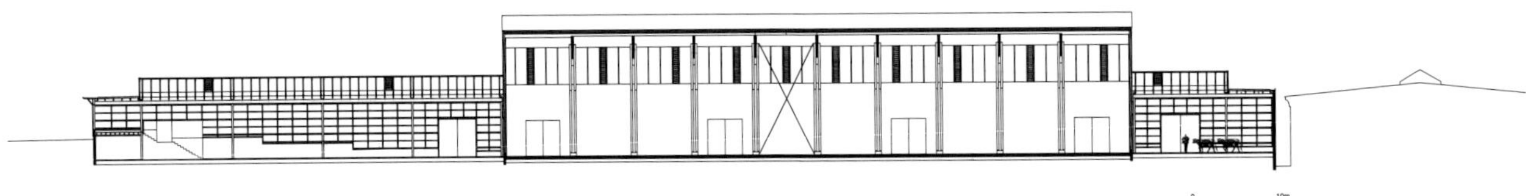

Long section through presentation room

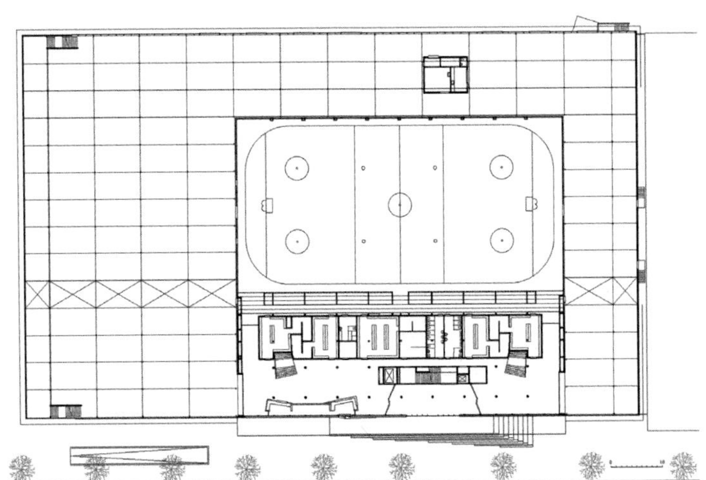

Entrance level

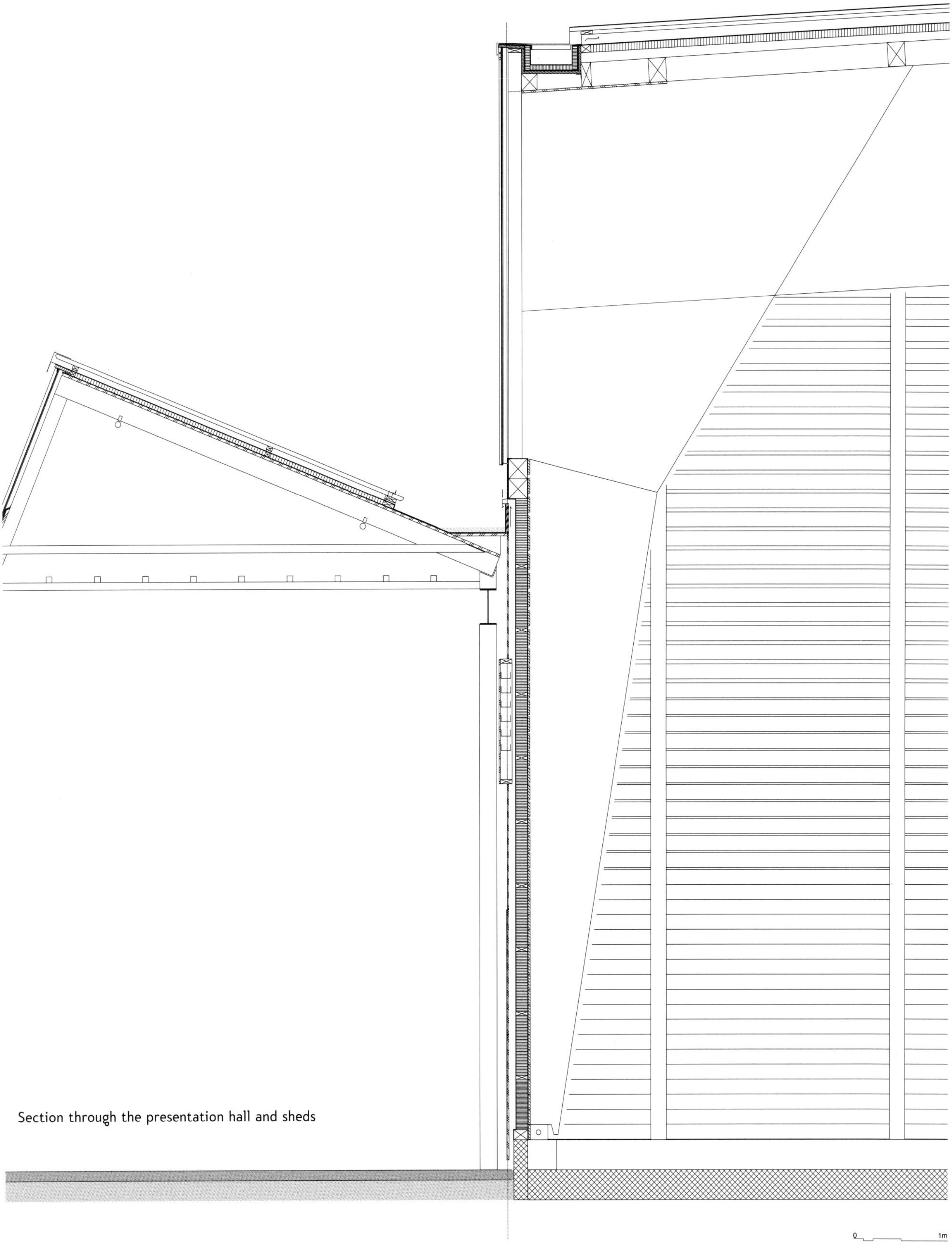

Section through the presentation hall and sheds

Previous situation

Situated alongside other property, on the corner of two roads giving access to the existing buildings on the site, the project reinterprets the theme of the house with a courtyard.

Formed from one enclosed space, the various volumes open onto three courtyards, the positions of which are determined by the presence of three different trees. To the south, the courtyard opens up to offer a glimpse of the lake. The mineral roofing and enclosed areas give the whole building the appearance of a block set down around the edges of the garden.

Future situation

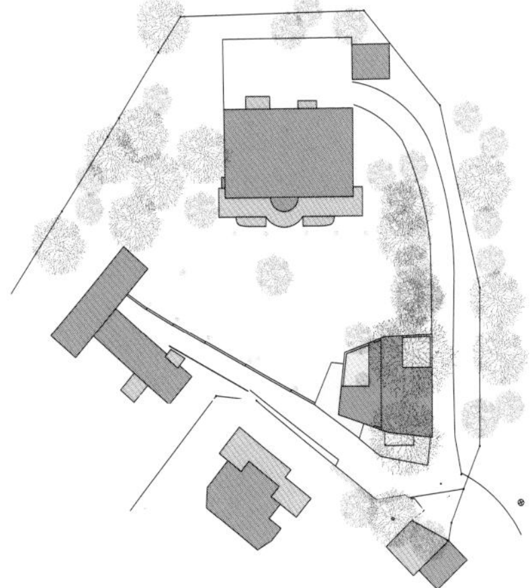

Site plan

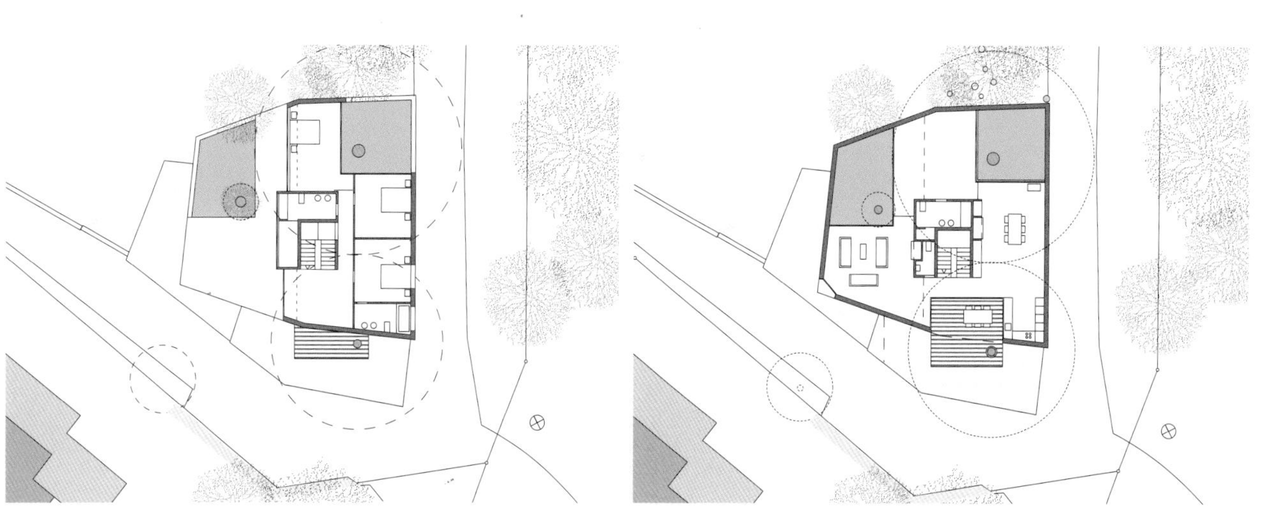

First floor plan

Ground floor plan

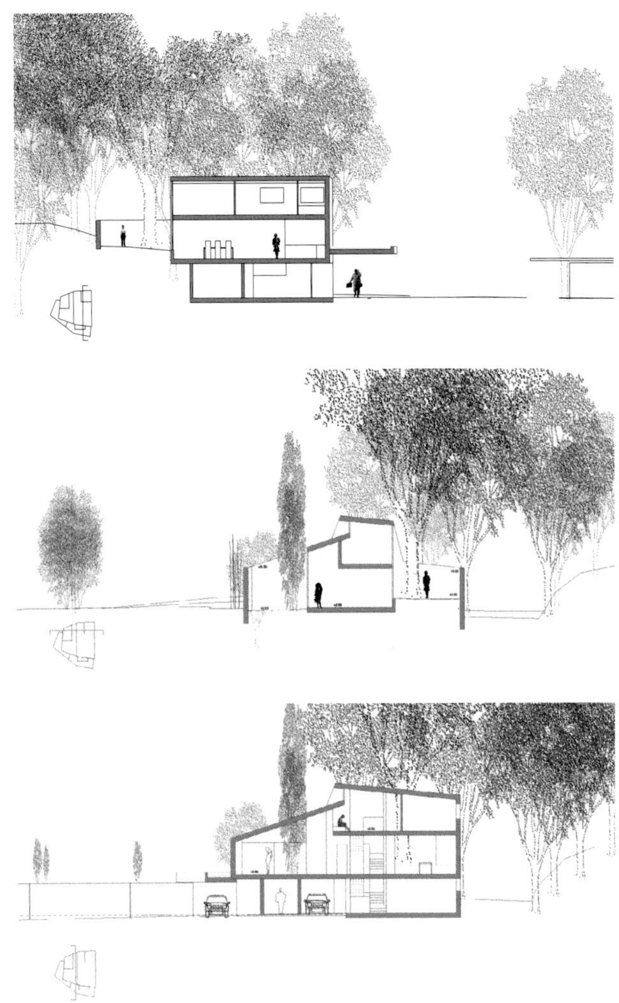

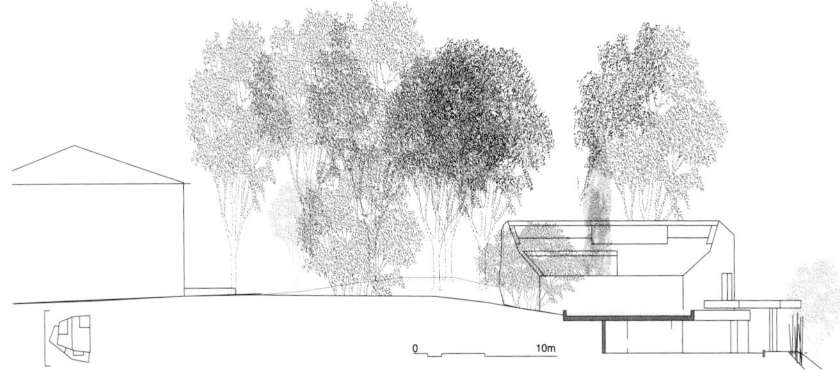

0   10m

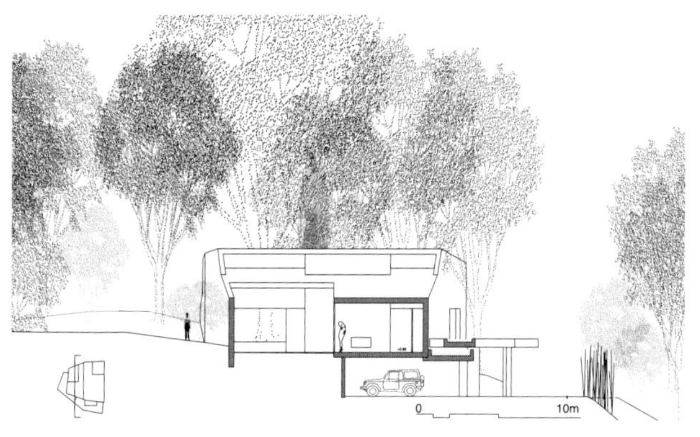

0
10m

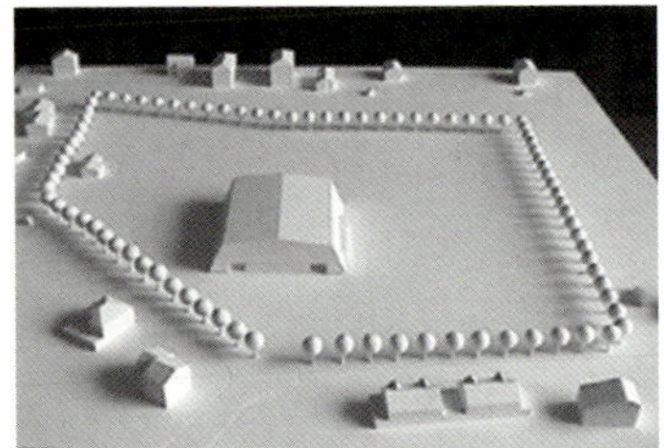

Set in the plain, this new public space is conceived as a meadow arranged to host fêtes and sporting events. The hall is conceived as a lightweight building set down on the meadow. Its expression is that of a lightweight public building of the residential area, seeking a volumetric relationship with the public buildings at the foot of the slope.

A light trap by day, a lantern at night, the hall becomes the symbol of the public space. Its double membrane allows its internal climate to be controlled and lets in a homogeneous light ideal for the practice of sport.

The apparently contradictory expression of a lightweight public building bases itself on the paradoxical qualities of contemporary glass:

- its apparent fragility;
- its resistance, its unchanging nature that gives it the status of contemporary stone.

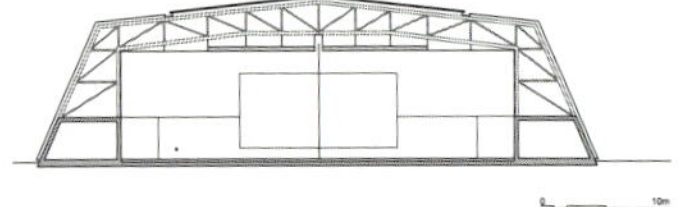

Section

Reference

Concept – site plan

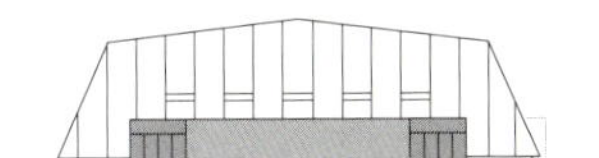

Entrance elevation

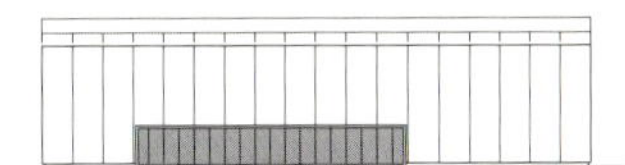

East elevation

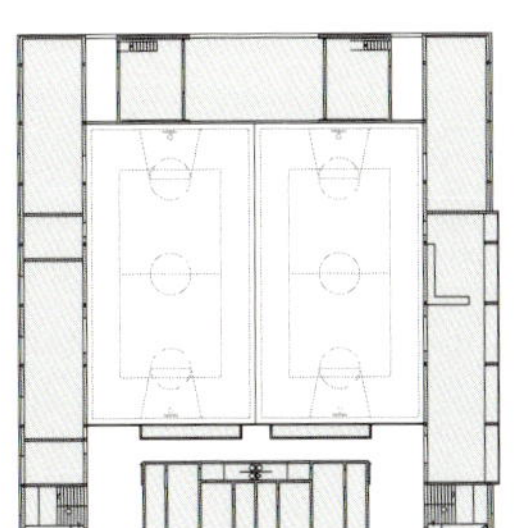

Entrance level

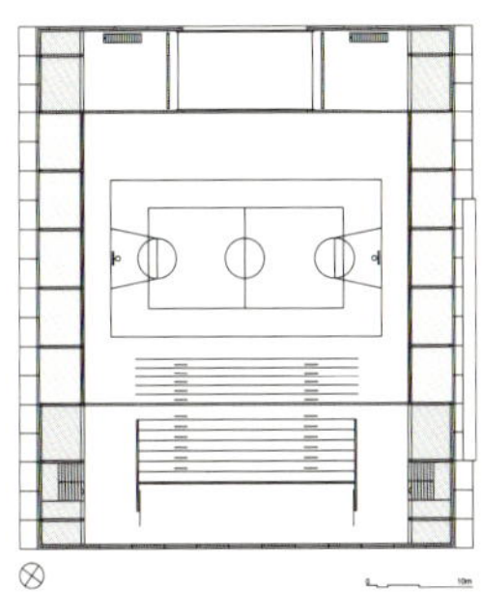

First floor plan

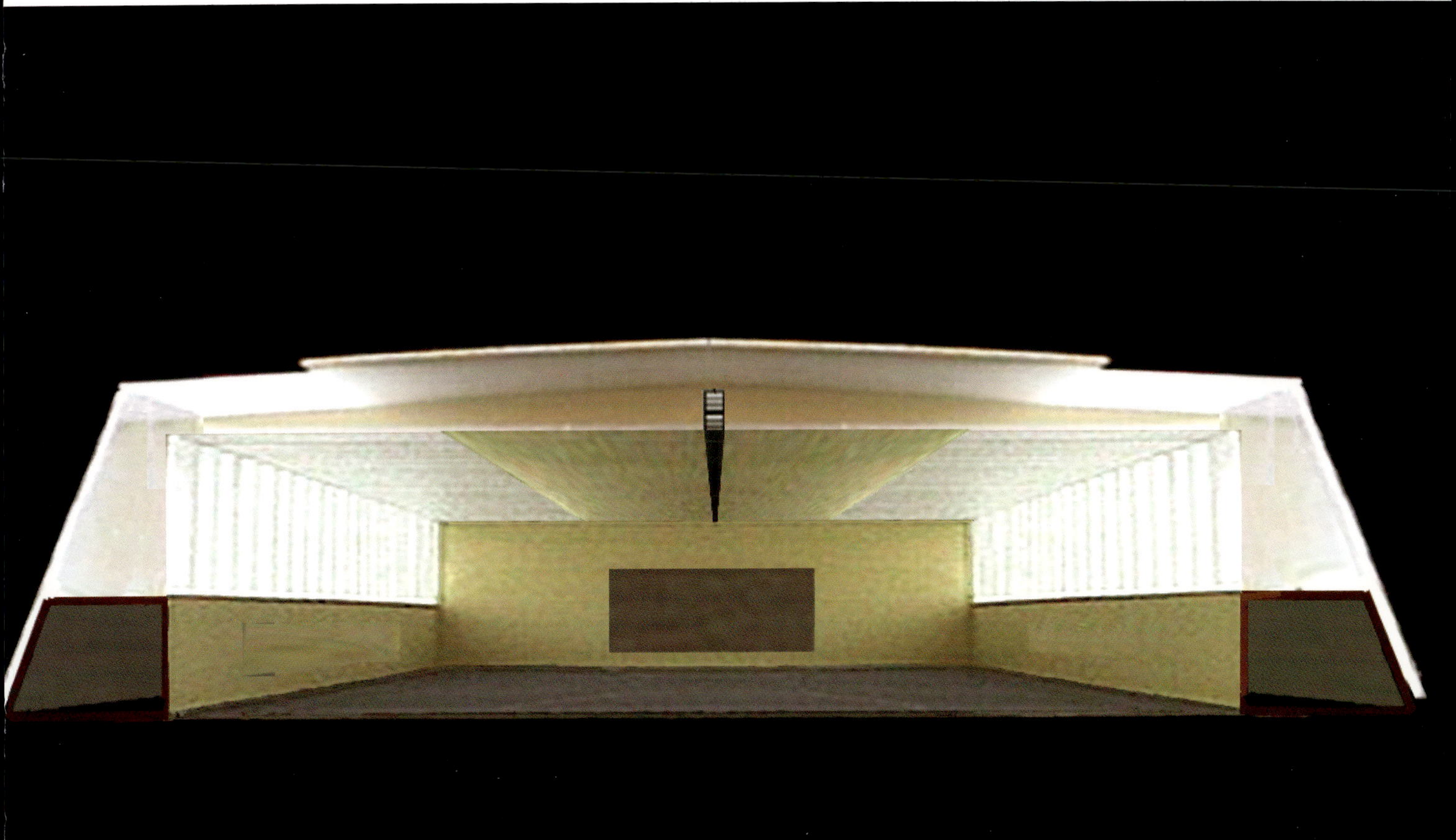

Urban concept

The plan proposes a building conceived as an aggregation of two pavilions in the park.

The fragmentation of the two volumes corresponds to the arborisation, but finds its raison d'être in the desire to create ideal natural light conditions for practising sport (bilateral lighting).

In order to create a lightweight public building, the project combines the qualities of wood and glass: inside, wood and polycarbonate define the smooth, standardised volume of a sports hall. Here the play area is in a bright, introverted space entirely its own.

Outside, the glass casing covers all the faces of the volume. This protective membrane detaches itself from the internal envelope by embracing the shape of the wooden frame. The resultant space is at the heart of the energy concept. As in old granaries, it forms a buffer zone that helps to conserve heat in the winter and provides good ventilation in the summer. A light trap by day, a lantern by night; solid and introverted by day, weightless and extraverted by night; in these plays of light, the pavilions become the symbol of the public space.

Energy concept

Winter: closed interstitial volume

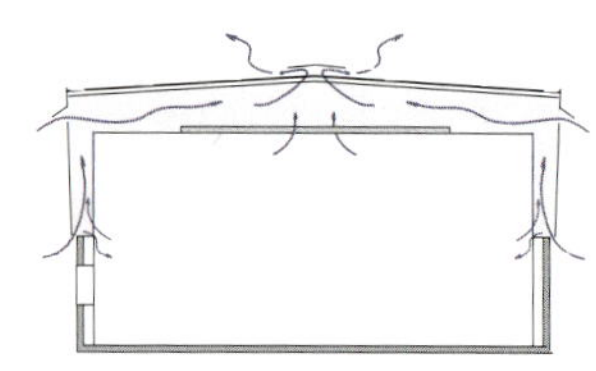

Summer: ventilated interstitial volume

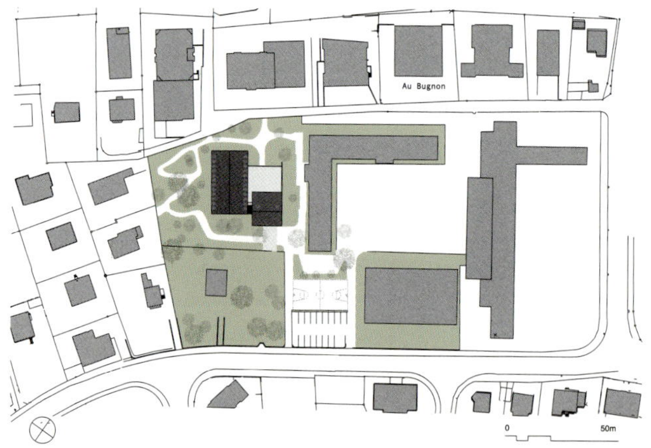

Site plan

Section through the gymnasium and the multifunctional rooms

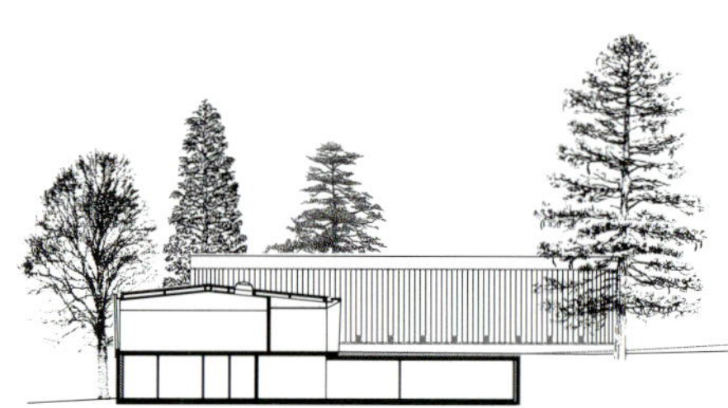

Section through the multifunctional room and east elevation

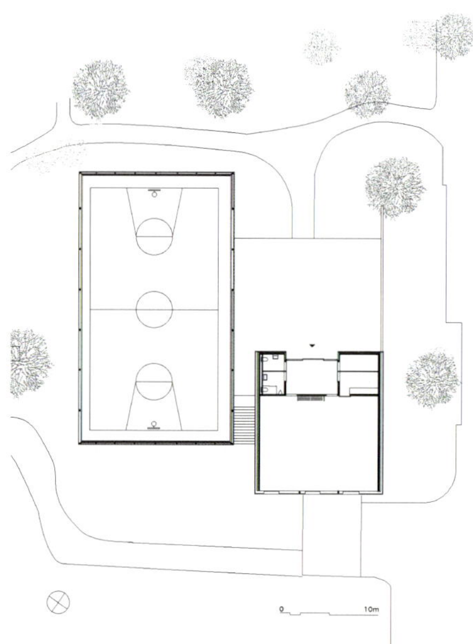

Entrance level

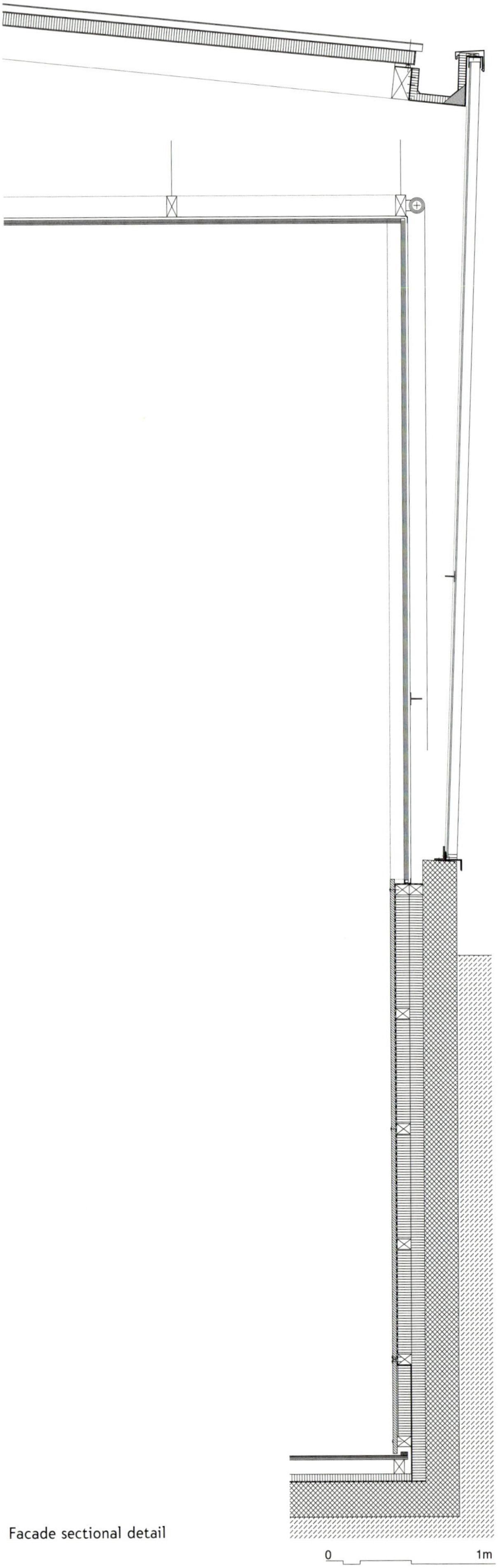

Facade sectional detail

0   1m

Situated in a very restricting environment (high-voltage line, buildings opposite, ventilation from the electrical sub-station) the project proposes the installation of a micro-perforated metal sheet redefining the relationships between the building and its immediate surroundings. This element creates a Faraday cage, eliminating harmful effects from the high-voltage lines; it serves as a sun protection to the south, a visual filter to the north and an air vent to the west for the electrical sub-station. This membrane unifies the whole building, creating plays of light between the interior and the exterior through its effect of semi-transparency.

Inside, the very high requirement for noise insulation between the consultation rooms has generated the arrangement, with each room forming an individual cell.

Principle of solar protection and visual filter

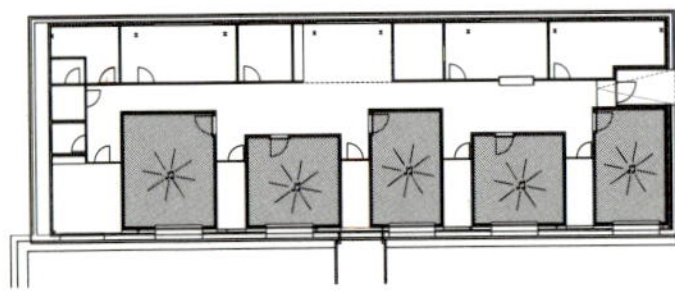

Soundproofing

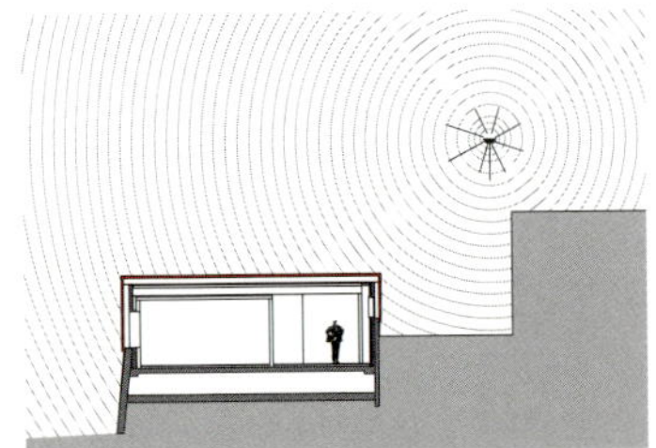

Faraday cage

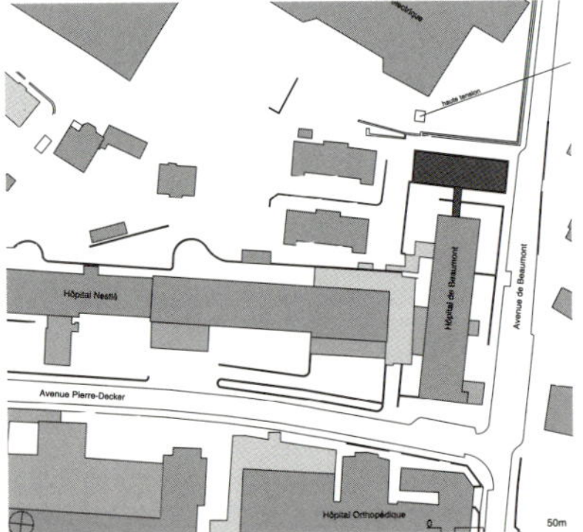

Site plan

CHUV - PHONIATRIE ET LOGOPEDIE

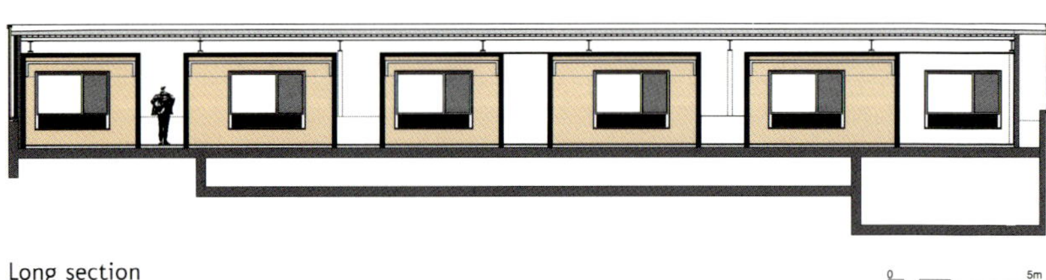

Long section

Entrance level

btx5

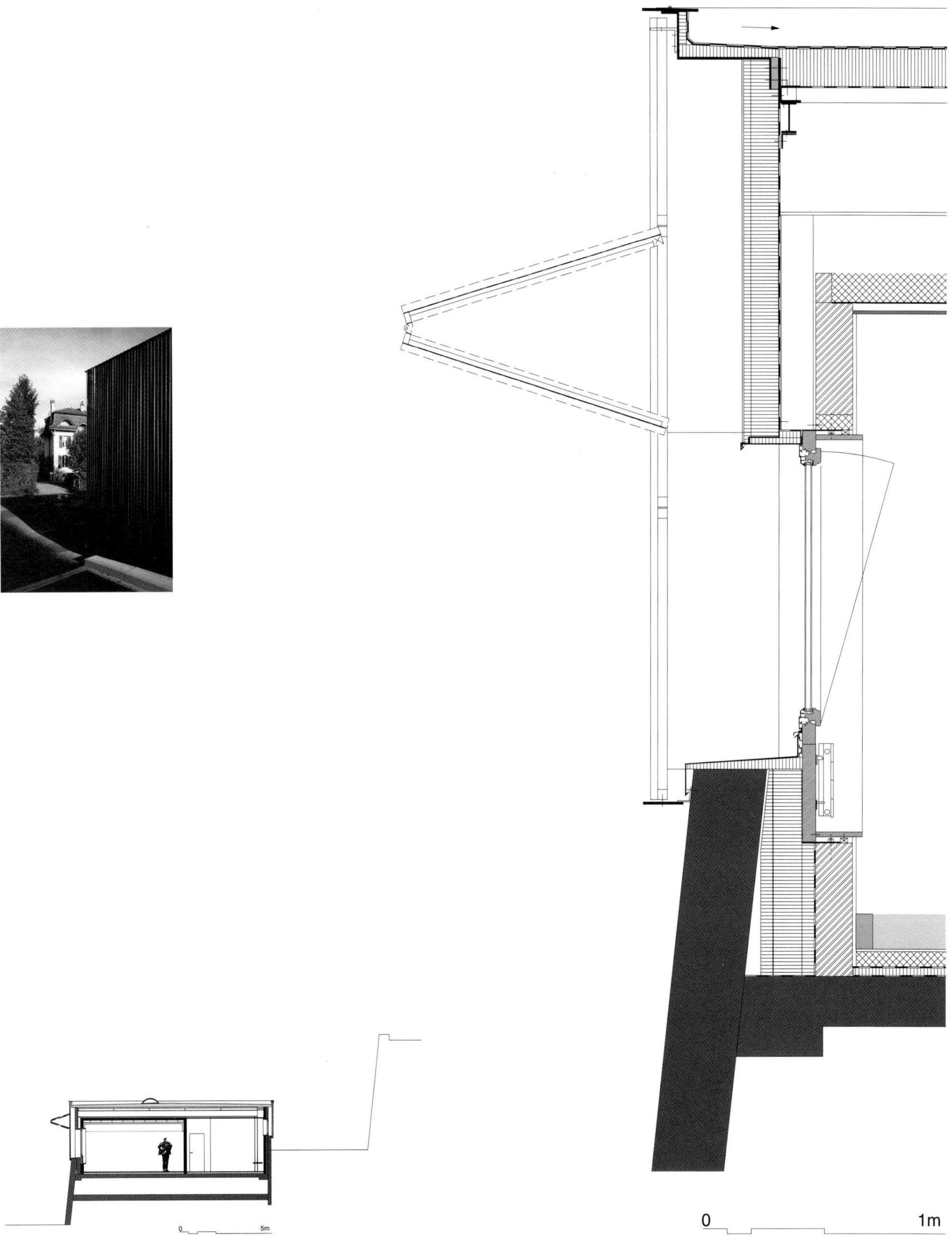

Cross section

South facade sectional detail

Faced with an obsolete building formed from various heterogeneous constructions, the project opts to recycle the existing infrastructures.

The integration of the new requirements is the pretext for renovation of the existing complex to form a new unified and coherent entity.

This idea of recycling is also symbolised by the materialisation of the mineral plinth uniting the old and the new buildings. The choice of prefabricated concrete serves two purposes: it made it possible to close off the building site so that the activity of the existing complex could be maintained, and it also made it possible to use recycled glass to form a mineral facade that opens up a dialogue with the Profilit glass of the neighbouring building.

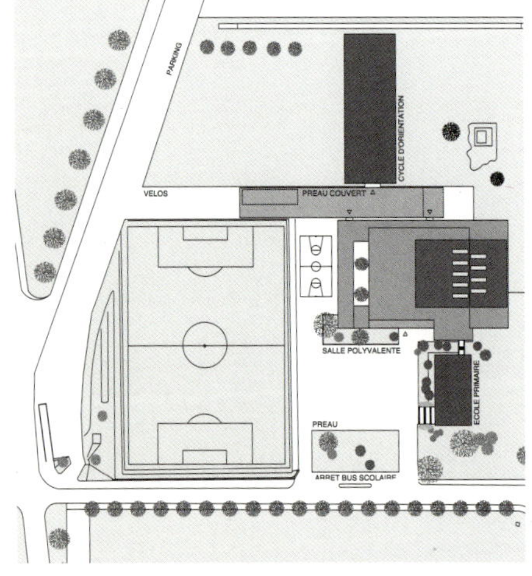

Site plan

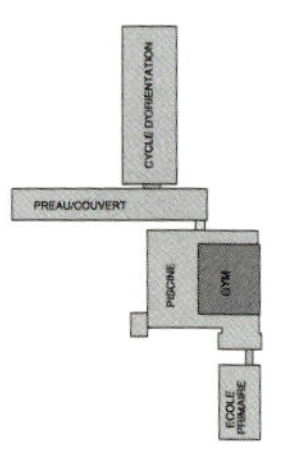

Existent

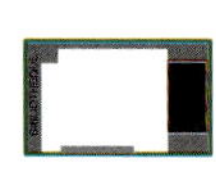

Addition

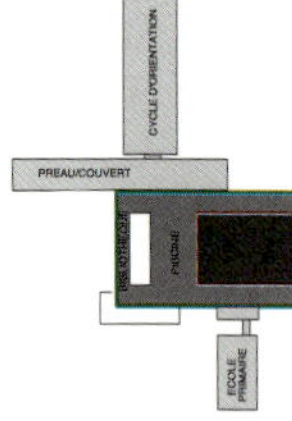

Configuration

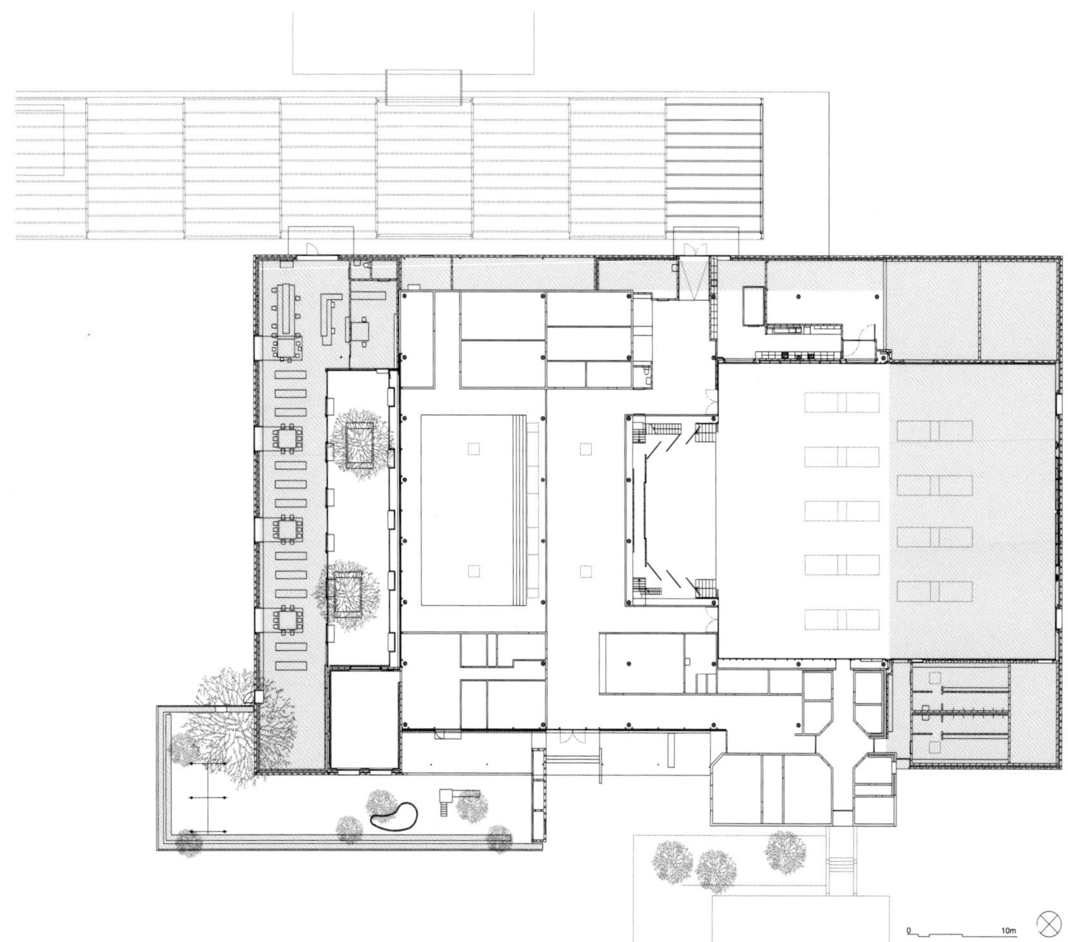

Entrance level

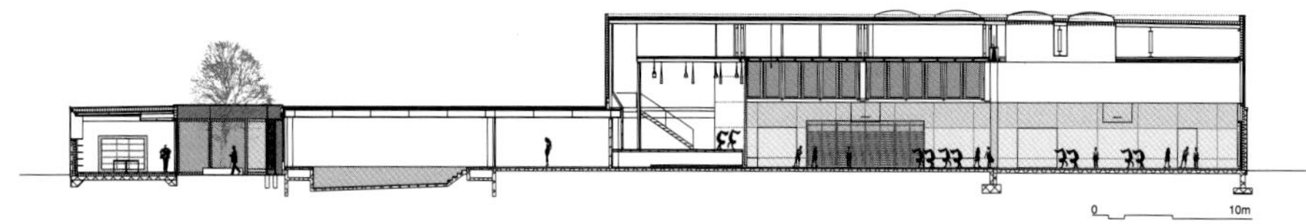

Section through the library, the patio and the gymnasium

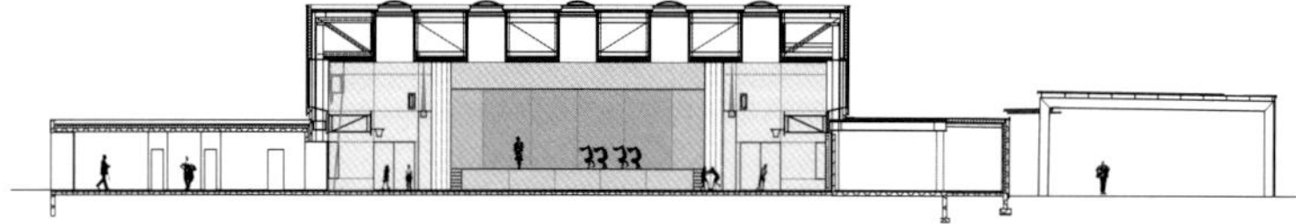

Transversal section through the gymnasium

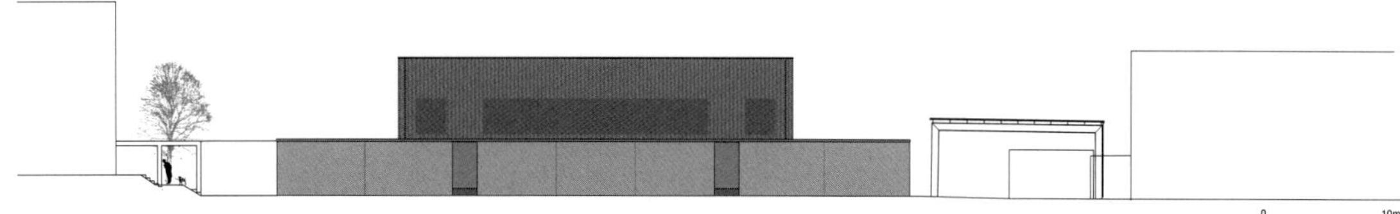

East elevation

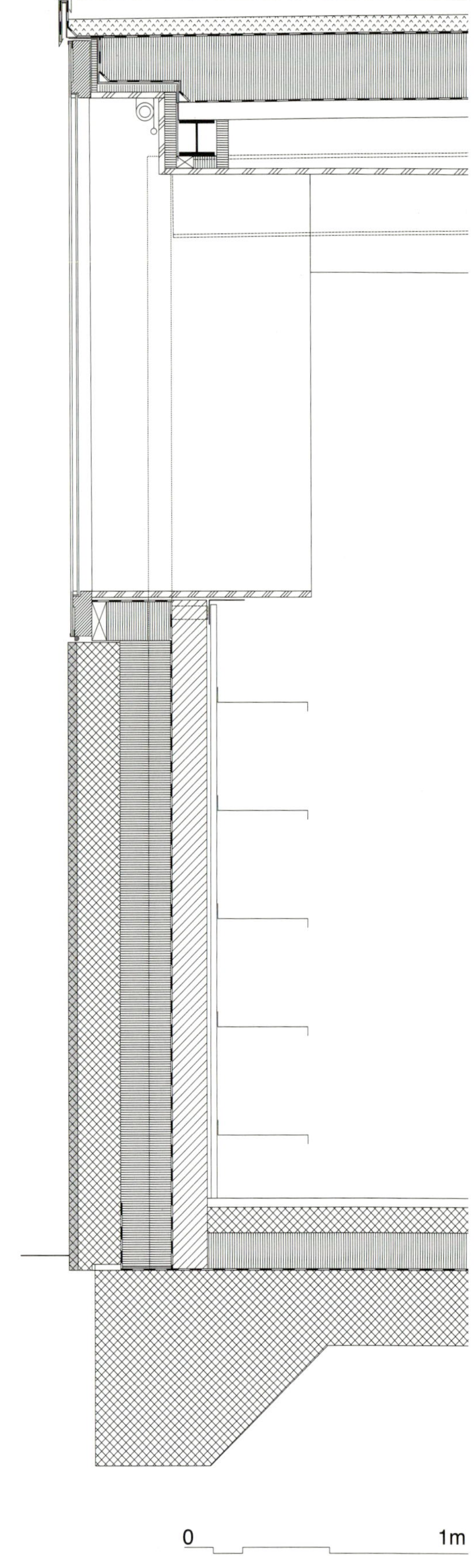

Library facade sectional detail

Given a brief concerning extremely in-troverted activities (concert, casino), and a building punctuated by moments of effervescence and periods of calm (casino), the project proposes an enclosed space that presents a facade of great serenity to the town at all moments. In the evenings, a column of light reveals the intense activity of the casino. It creates tension in the mono-lith which is at first sight immutable and extracts the theatre from the routine life of the town.

The foyer seeks contact with the rock, both through the views towards the peaks (skylights) and through the hall-way leading out onto the covered ter-race outside, offering a complementary scene opposite the rock.

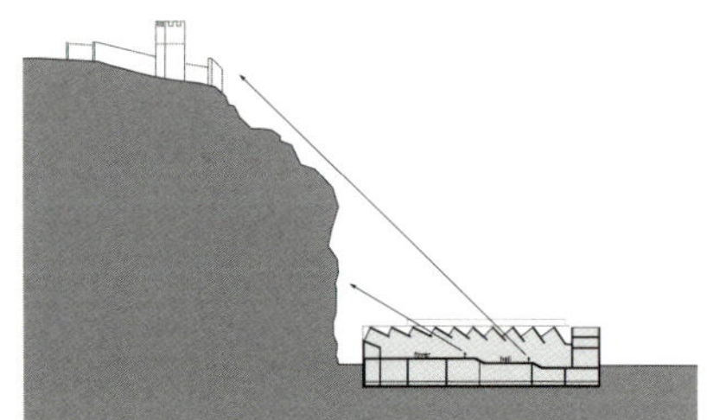

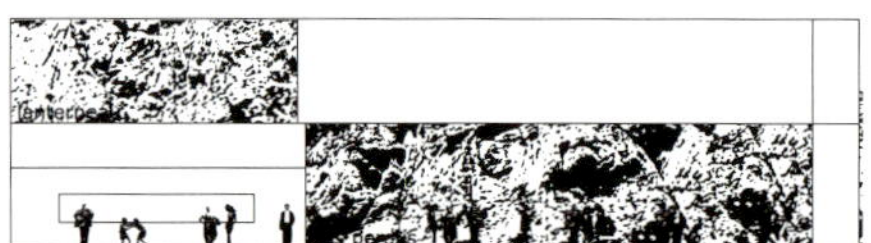

Concept section through foyer

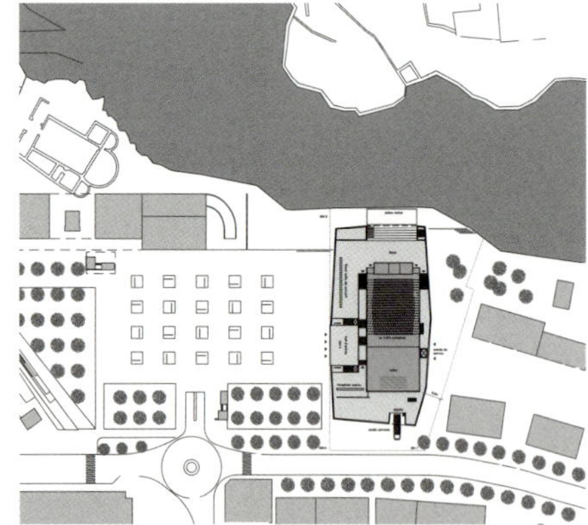

Site plan

Entrance elvation

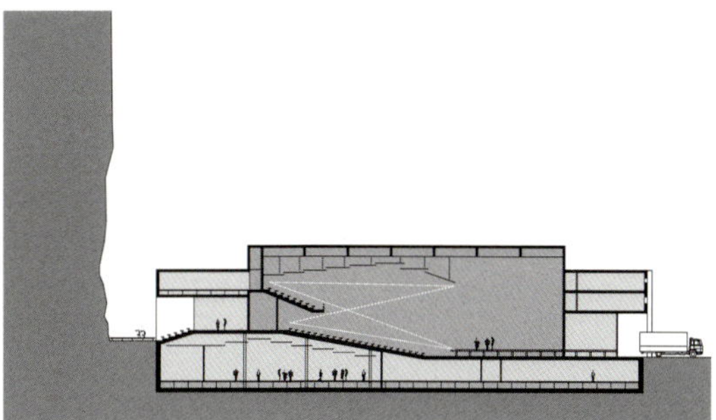

Long section

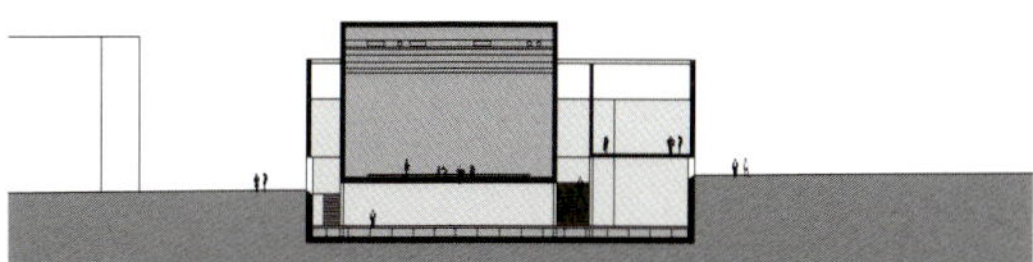

Cross section

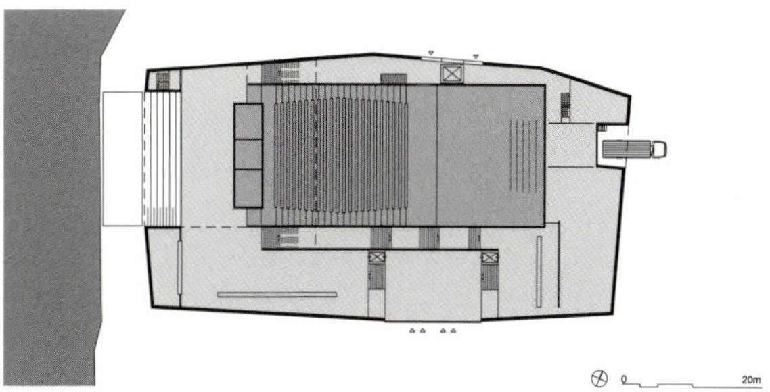

Entrance level

The project sits on a hill slope, previously used as a vineyard, overlooking the lake. At the top of the hill a mansion dominates a garden that was never landscaped.

To build in the "garden" led logically to the theme of "building" the garden. The positioning of the project therefore defined the hill. The retaining wall creates the garden terrace and leads on to the new building's entrance. The new building leans against the slope and is articulated in two volumes, each of which welcomes a living space.

One, perpendicular to the slope ends the garden retaining wall and offers its roof as a "belvedere" for the stately home. The other follows the site contours and creates the entrance space to the new building. The two volumes mask the view to the lake panorama and orchestrate an entry scenario.

Inside the apartments, the living area is on the upper entry level, offering in this way the most impressive views of the lake directly related to the entrance. The bedrooms are placed on the lower floor with the desire to focus in a more intimate manner on the close proximity of the orchard and the forest, thereby distancing the big panorama.

The architectural language and devices used look to a direct relationship of the understanding of materials, climate, seasons, and the passage of each hour of the day with the wish to unite daily rhythm with the natural environment.

The use of exposed concrete is a studied choice given the project objectives. The need for a retaining wall is to span the long horizontal opening and also because it marries well with our vision for this type of dwelling as a place where one puts down roots, a place to which one returns continually.

Site section and plan

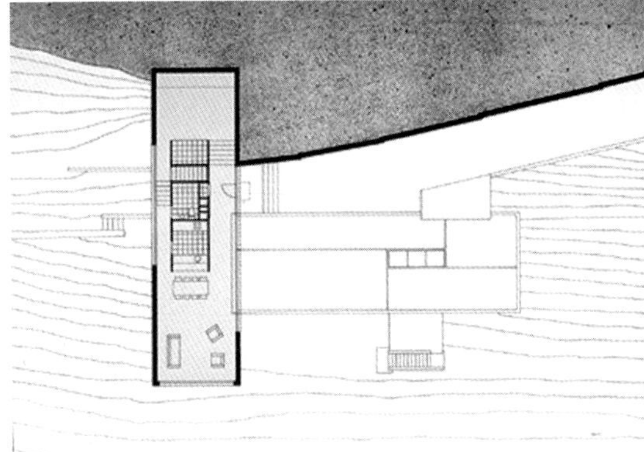

Upper floor plan

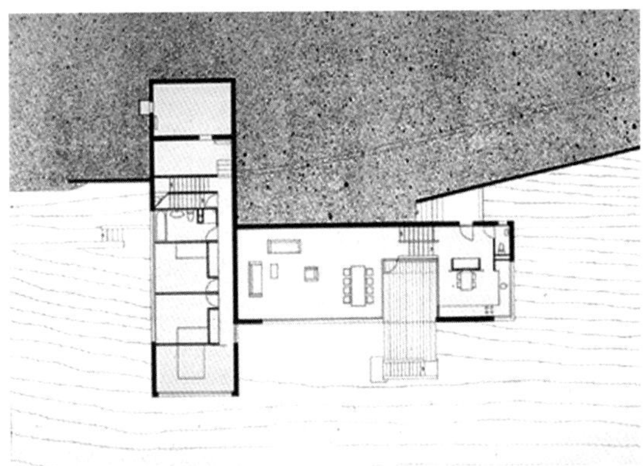

Ground floor plan

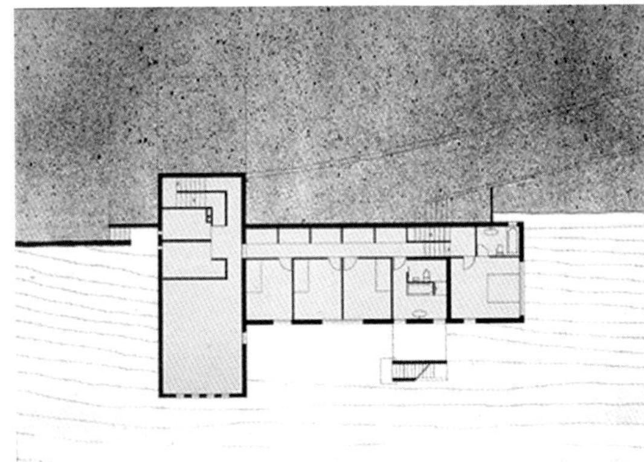

Lower floor plan

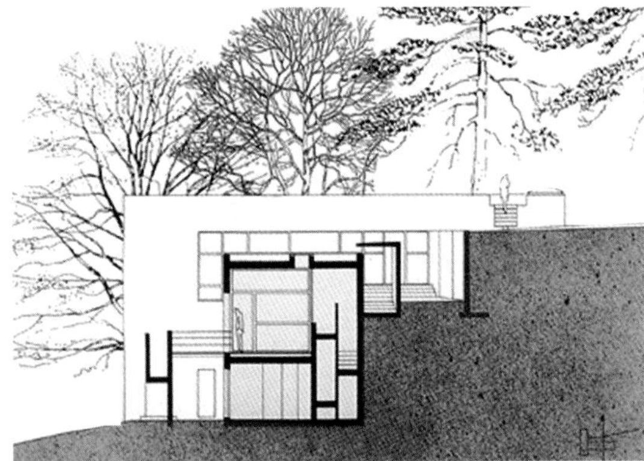

Section south elevation

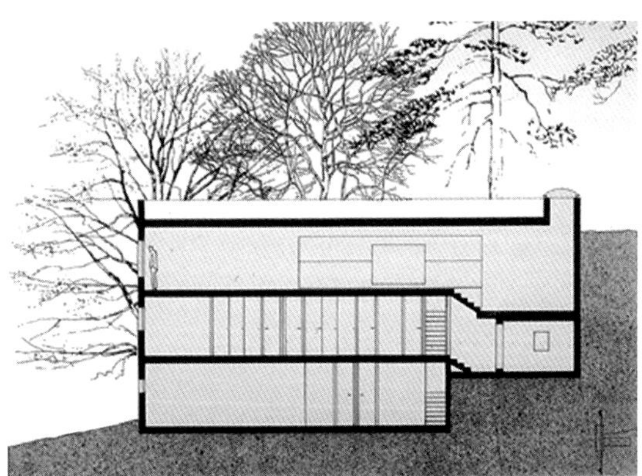

Long section north apartment

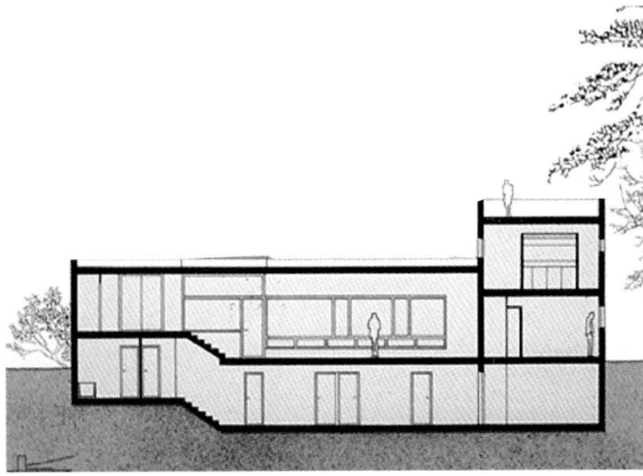

Long section south apartment

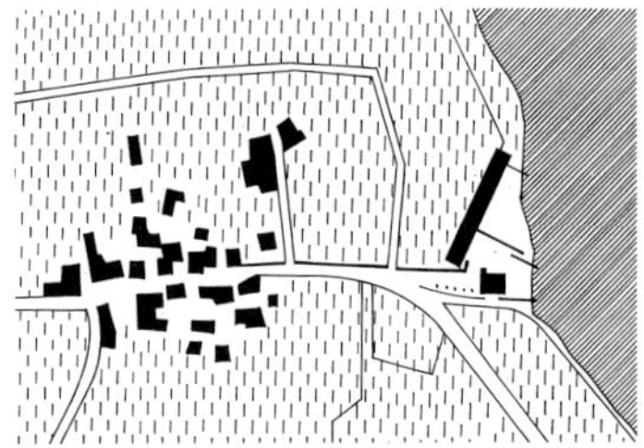

Previous situation

Previous situation

View of the entrance

The project is rooted in a unique site characterised by the omnipresence of rock, vineyards, an existing school building and a dyke. A wall was built shortly after the construction of the old school with the material brought down by a freak flood and where the ground floor of the school was buried on two sides.

By locating the new school on the line of the old dyke, the old school becomes an even stronger reference and clarifies its relation to the village and its *genius loci*. The wall which defines the entrances to the school complex is built in a contextual continuity of the neighbouring vineyards reusing the stones of the old dyke.

By its form, volume and positioning, the new building defines the boundary of the vineyards and creates a reference space uniting all the elements of the composition. This protected and mineral space establishes assured relationships with the old school and the plain and is structured in two parts: the lower part is a public space giving access to the classroom building, gymnasium and the existing building. The upper part offers a "suspended" playground accessible directly from the classroom corridors.

The linear form of the new building guarantees each classroom extended views of the vineyards and a direct contact with the playground and the rock. The classroom arrangement was conceived at one with the wish to orientate the building structure naturally with the logical position of the blackboard. In conclusion, the reorganised and extended school complex forms a new composition where the existing school becomes the representative element.

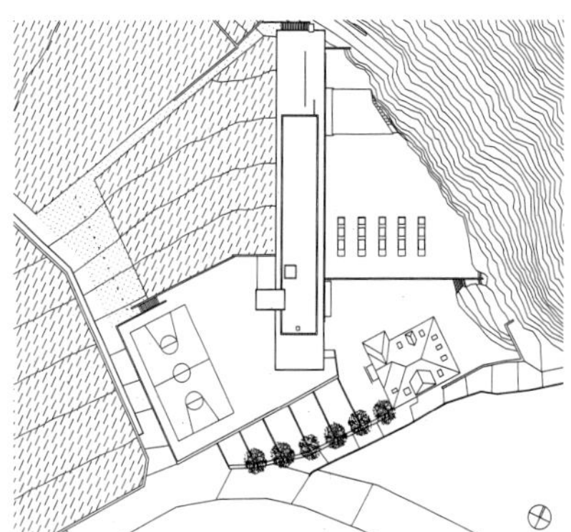

Site plan

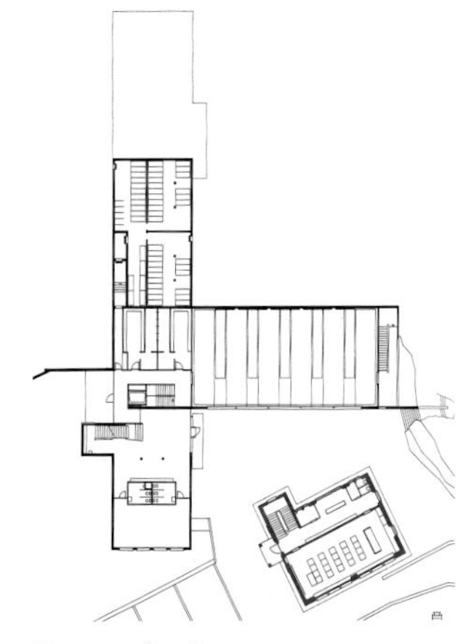

Entrance level

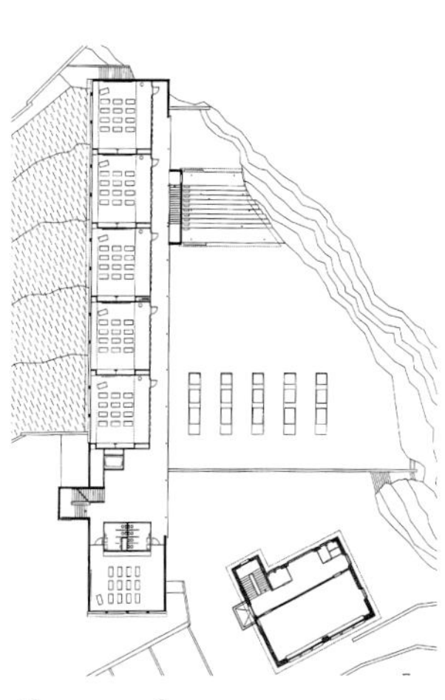

Classroom plan

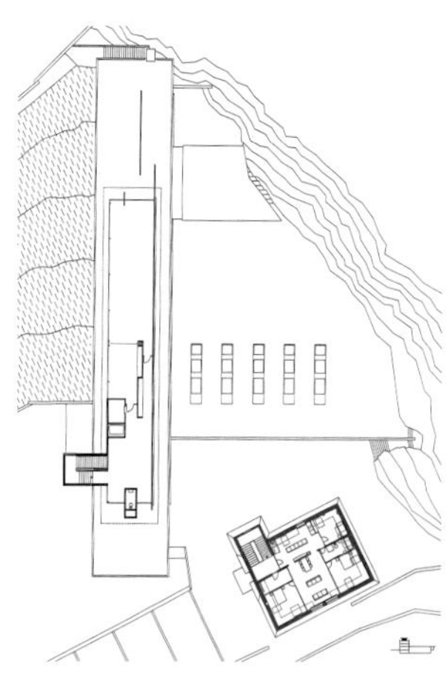

Roof plan

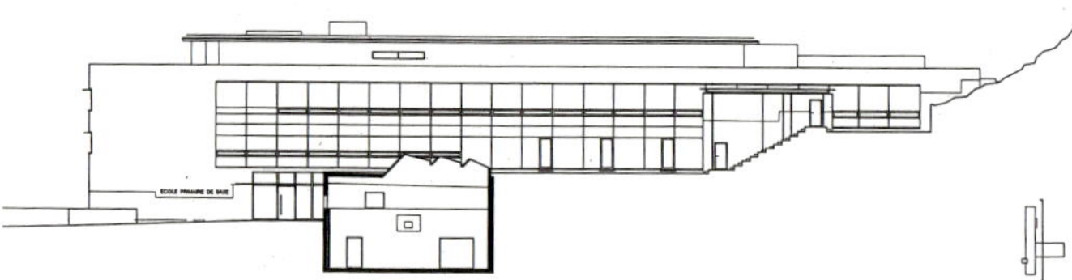

East elevation section through the gymnasium

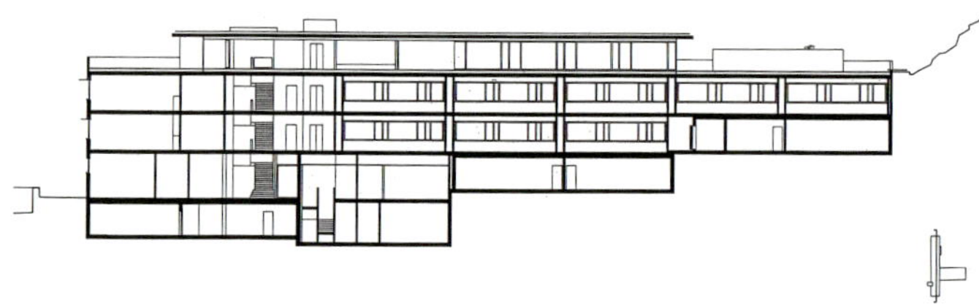

Long section

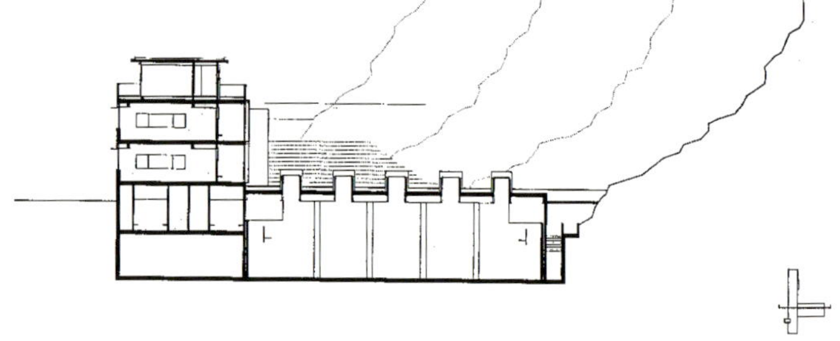

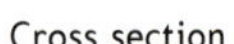

Cross section

Interior of the gymnasium

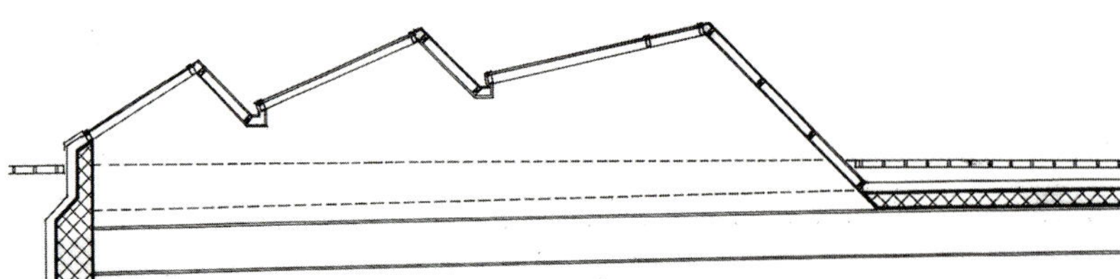

Detail section through the skylights

The project proposes the conversion into three apartments of a 19th-century farmhouse now swallowed up by the town.

The two lower apartments have a direct relationship with the garden. On the other hand, the project creates new relationships between the garden and the apartment on the two upper floors. To the north, an external wooden staircase connects the kitchen with the garden. To the south, the existing narrow balcony is extended by a projecting seat embedded in the new parapet. Inside, the conversion concentrates towards the north (inclusion of the internal staircase and kitchen) in order to retain the character of the main existing spaces to the south.

Site plan

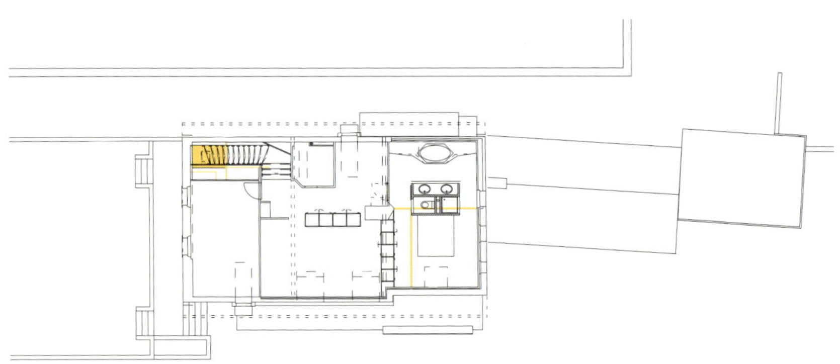

Attic plan

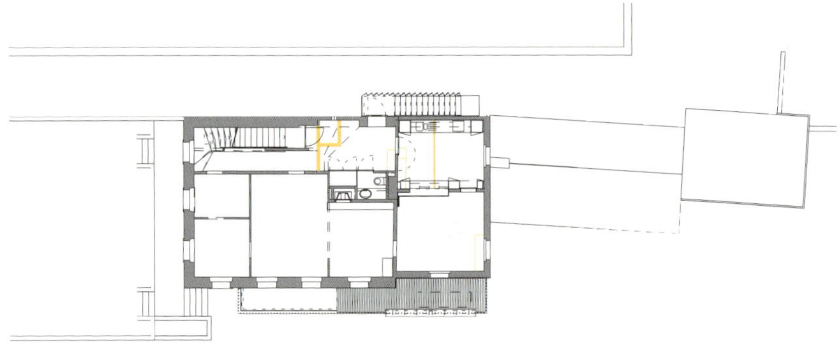

First floor plan

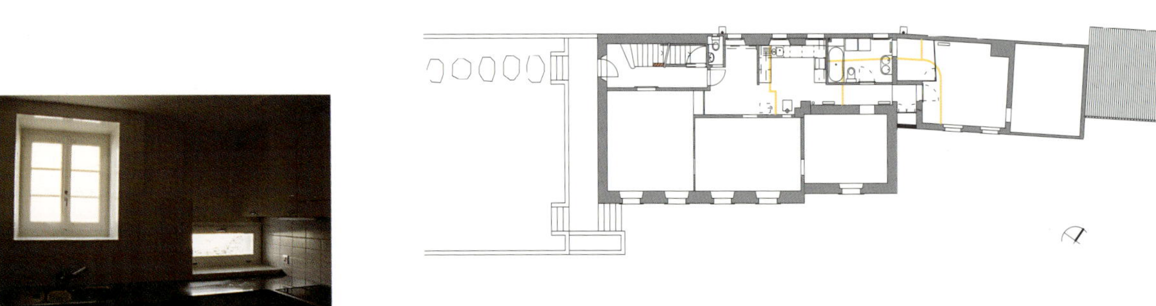

Entrance plan

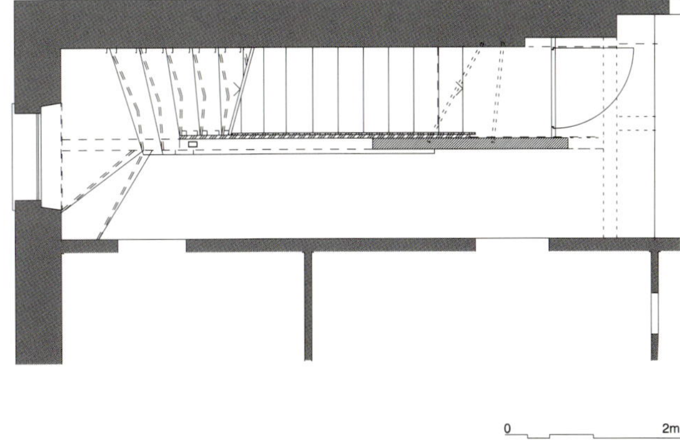

New staircase plan

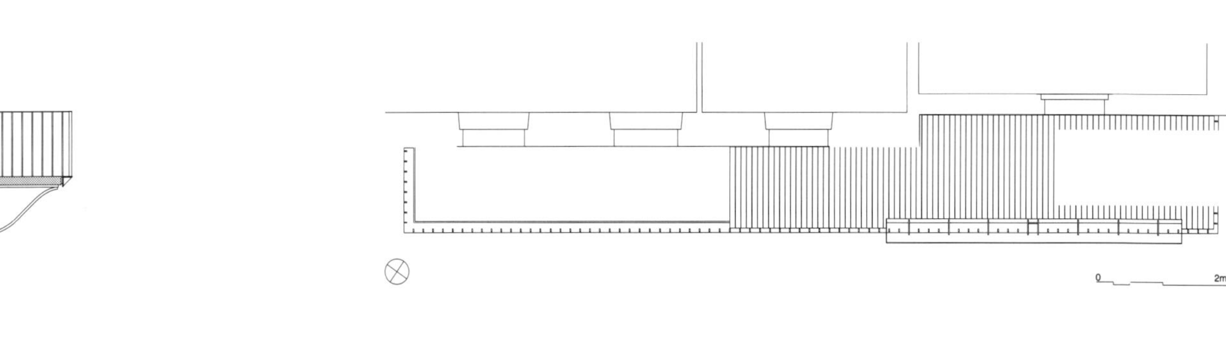

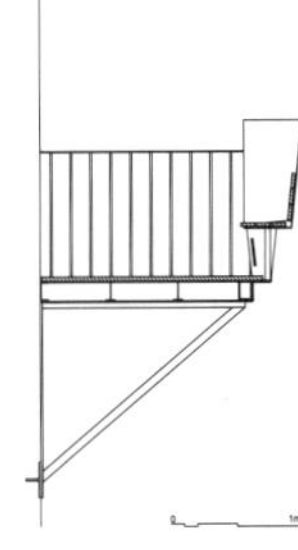

Section, plan and elevation of the enlarged balcony

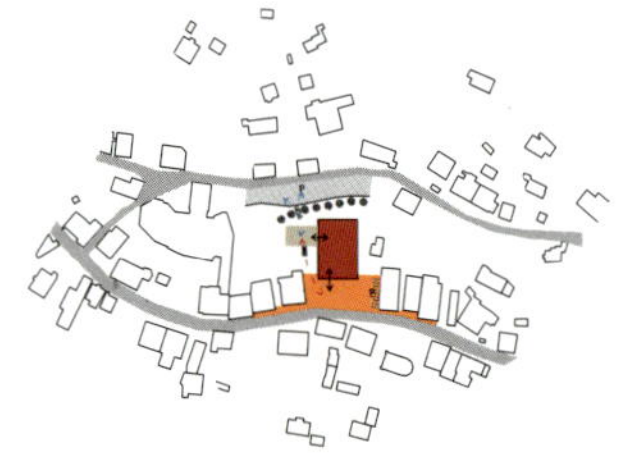

Site plan

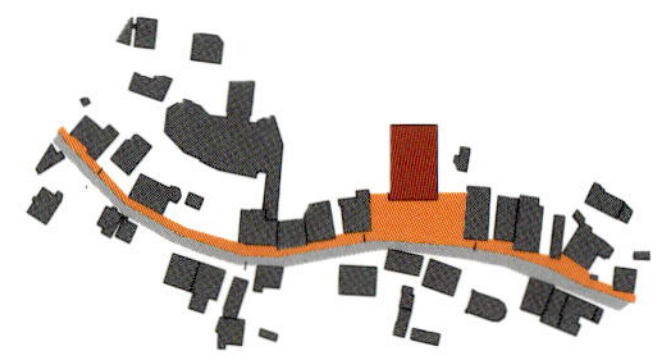

Interior view of the gymnasium

Positioned set back from the main road, the building defines the village square. Its volume enters into a relationship with the large built volumes all around it. The main facade resembles the entrance of the village hall and the entrance of the shopping centre.

Further up the slope, its roof becomes a facade set down in the orchard. It opens up a dialogue with the roofs that form the silhouette of the village.

In contrast with the simplicity of the whole building, the entrance portico is formed of a double skin, with the outer glass skin protecting the carpentry and the device for offering sun protection or for darkening the glass.

The building's facade expresses the festive spirit of a village hall.

The question of sustainable development is not a main theme in itself, but it is integrated, like other themes, at all levels of the design (volumetry, position, construction, use). For example, the building seeks to assert its volume, with the aim of giving structure to the public space: this choice also makes it possible to define a relationship with the earth surrounding the buried construction works, avid consumers of grey energy (excavations and works in concrete) and to favour building in wood.

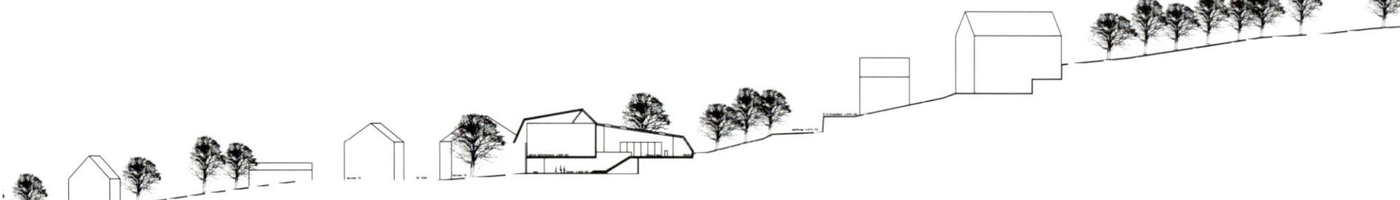

Section

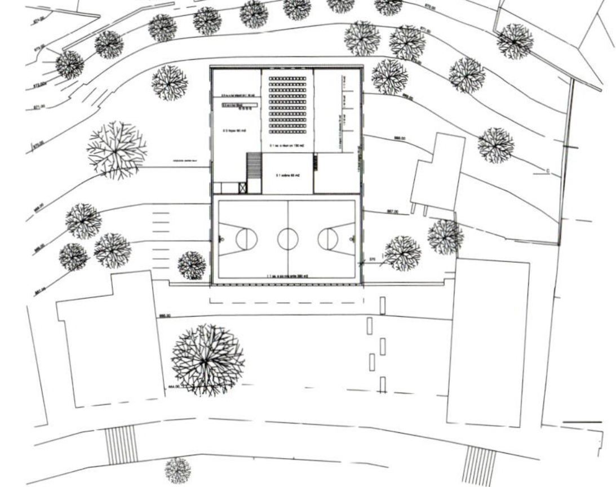

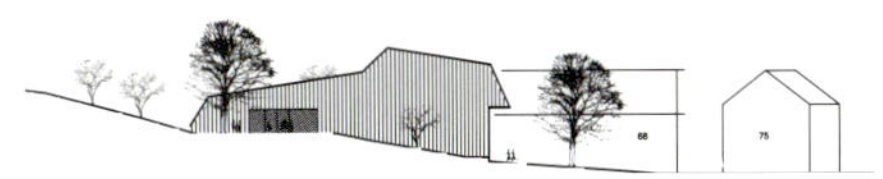

West elevation

First level

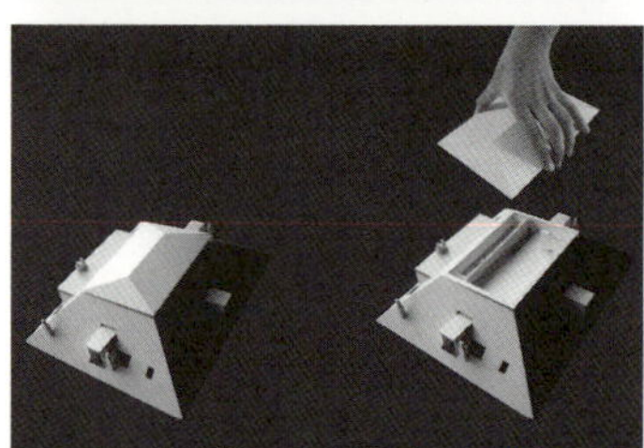

This project proposes the creation of an apartment in the loft of a 19th-century urban house. Situated to the north of a very busy main road, this building benefits from panoramic views of the lake.

In order to give the dwelling a generous external space that is protected from the noise and takes full advantage of the view, the plan exploits the geometry of the existing roof to add a new terrace.

Inside, the conversion concentrates on creating one large room, the space of which is defined by the tension between the view out over the lake and the light flooding in through the new skylight.

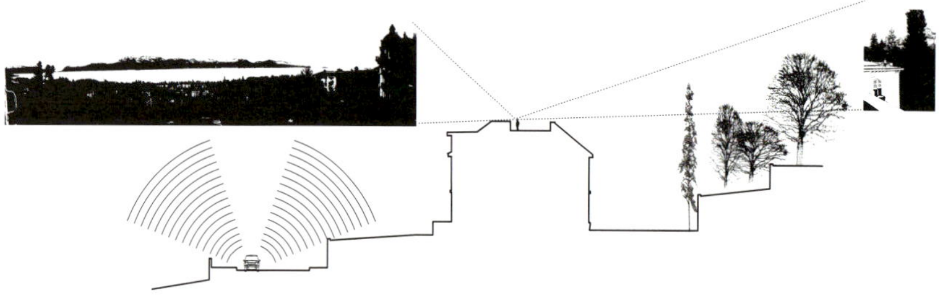

Conceptual section

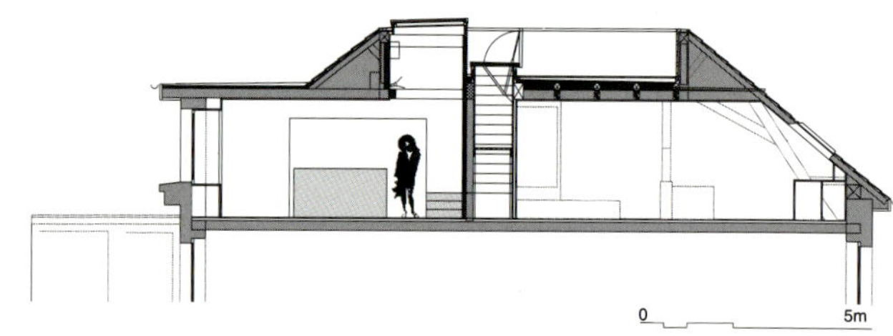

Section through the living room and the stained glass

Attic floor plan

Flat roof plan

The situation of the building and the treatment of the exterior are arranged in such a way as to make a focal point of the tall lime tree present on the site. Higher up the slope, the covered playground, the special classrooms and the library form a pole of activity beneath the lime tree in direct contact with the footpath connecting Chisaz to Marcolet. The arrangement reveals the topography of the site. Further down the slope, the classrooms and the sports hall form a mural plinth in contact with the ground. The coarse casting and the deep embrasures of the classroom windows reinforce the anchoring of the plinth in the soil, while protecting the classrooms from a direct view of the entrance spaces.

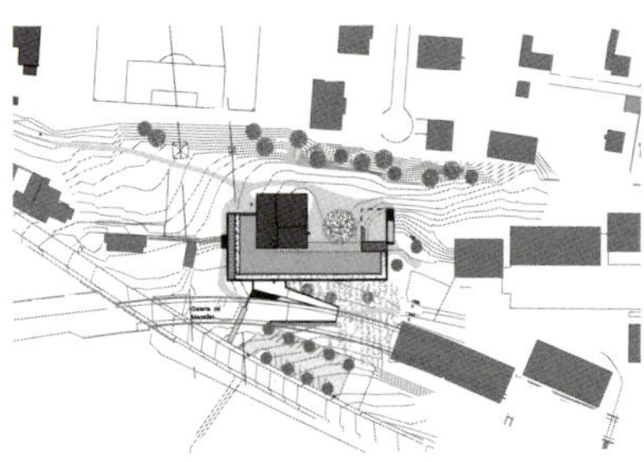

Site plan

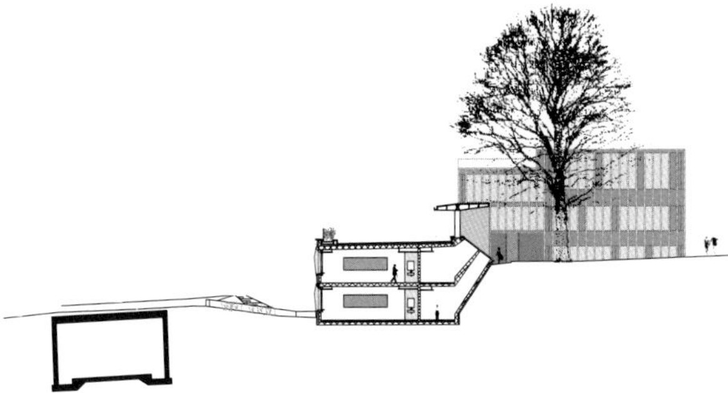

Section through the classrooms and the ground

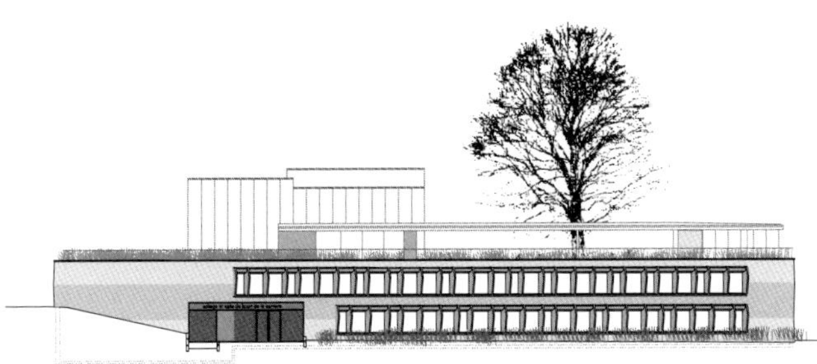

West elevation

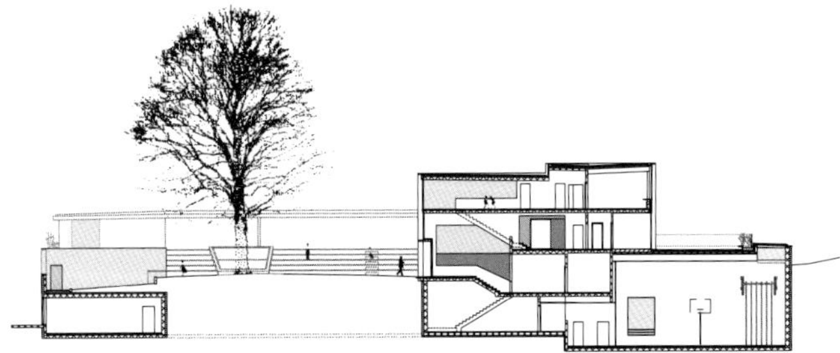

Transversal section through the gymnasium

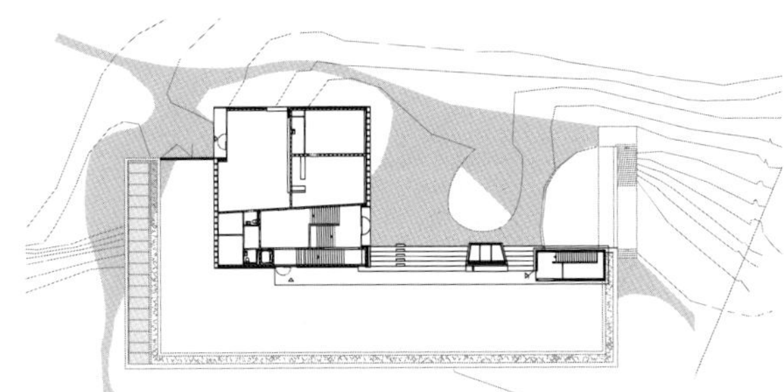

Library and playground level

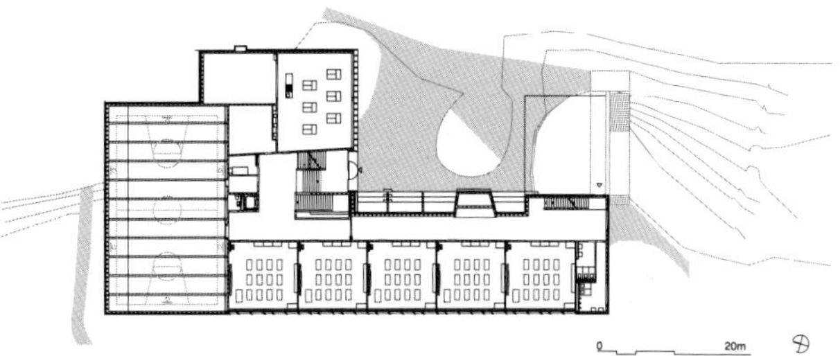

Classrooms level

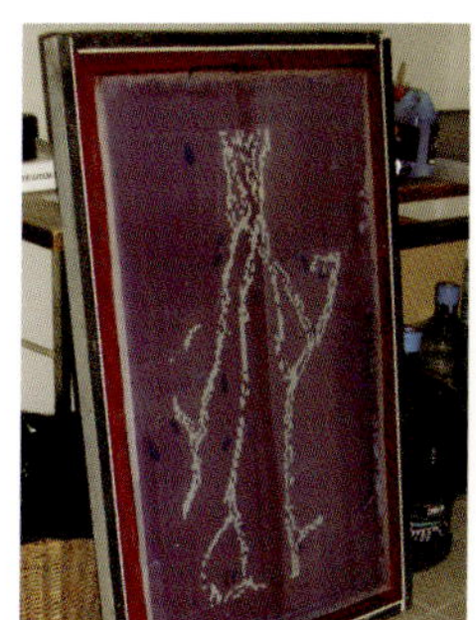

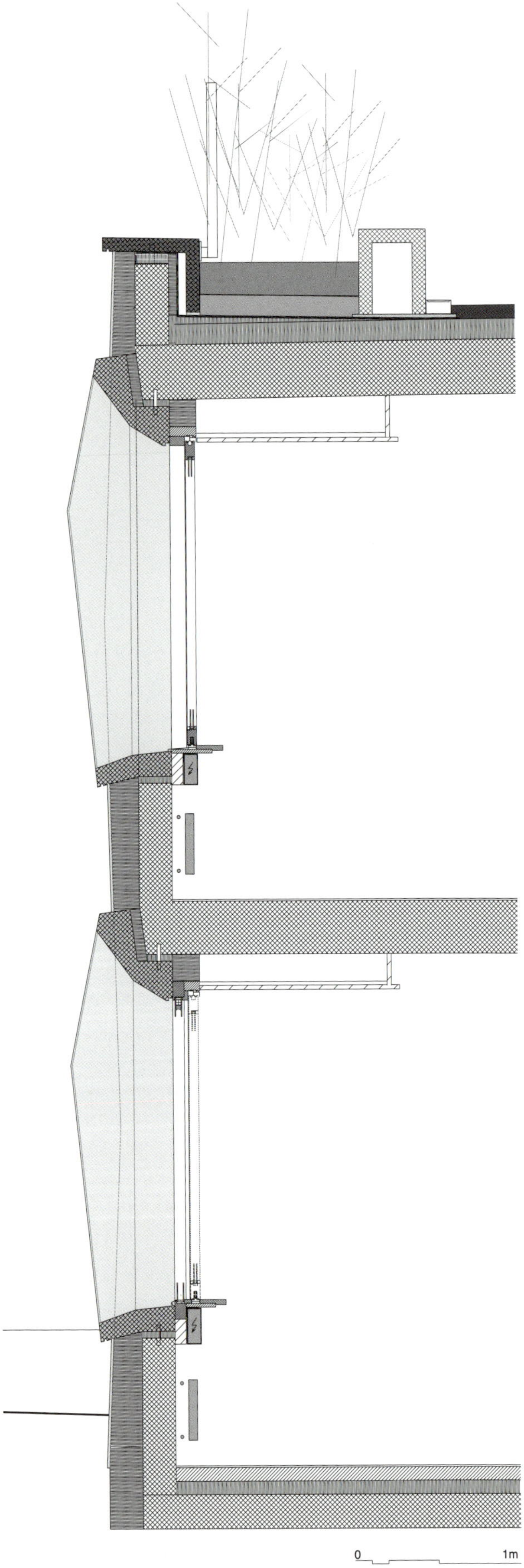

West facade sectional detail

Development of
la Place du Pré de Foire

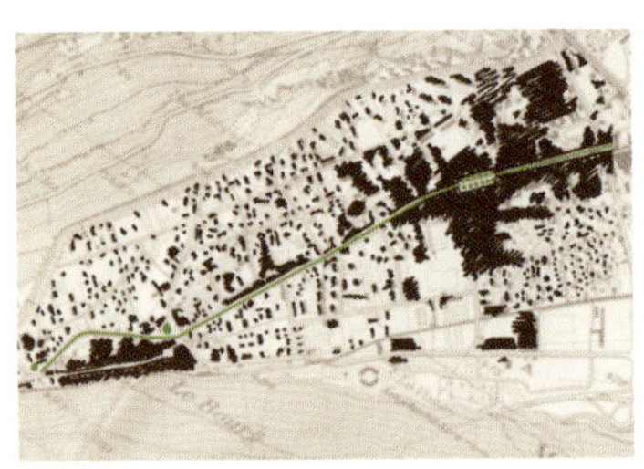

To complement the qualities of the market square (urban mineral void) the project proposes to define the Place du Pré de Foire by building a vegetal volume, a focal point able to restore the spatial unity destroyed by the extension of the avenue du Grand-St-Bernard. Historically, the Place du Pré de Foire is a functional complement to the market town. The project reinterprets this reality on the basis of current needs: complementarity of pedestrians/vehicles.

On the opposite side of the central square, where the plane trees have been pruned, there is a group of plane trees planted close together. The group grows untrimmed and untrained, but its shape derives from the geometry of the plantation and not from its annual trimming. The plan is to plant 28 *Platanus acerifolia,* six to eight metres high. Their crowns develop four metres from the ground. Eventually the trees will reach a height of 30 to 40 metres, forming a visual landmark. The confusion of foliage will grow out to a width of around eight metres. On the ground, a permeable membrane will allow gaseous exchanges to take place and rainwater to infiltrate. In the 250 cubic metre plantation trench for the 28 trees, an aerated earth/stone mix will encourage the diffusion of the water that is present in abundance in the subsoil.

The surfaces of the vehicle accesses and the pavements are covered in a coating of grit-blasted macadam. They define the transition between the mineral world of the town and the vegetal ambience of the Place du Pré de Foire. On the ground in the square, accompanying the vegetal volume, a coating of permeable stabilised gravel will serve as a reminder of the historically rural nature of the place. At night, by lighting the volumes of the plane trees from inside, they will be transformed into vegetal lanterns.

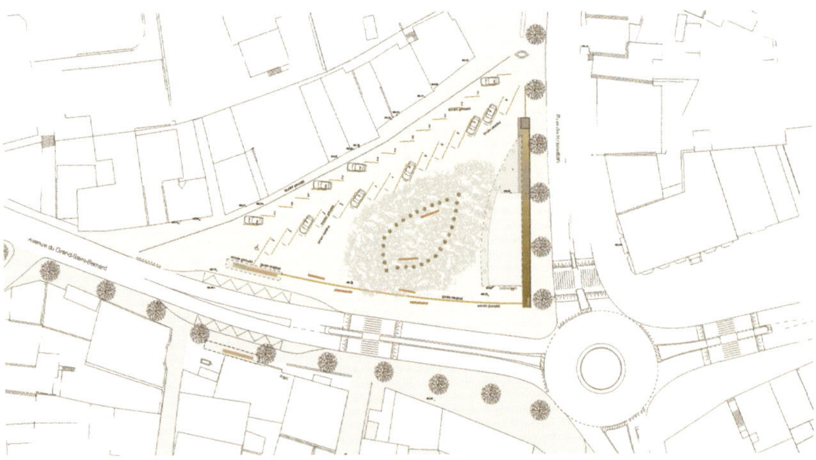

Site plan

View from the avenue du Grand-St-Bernard

Permanent places
Ephemeral places

	Project	Realisation
SIA Pavilion , Martigny	1994	1994
Olympic village study, Sion	1997	
Plan for the National Swiss Library, Berne	2001	
New museum of modern art, Lausanne	2004	

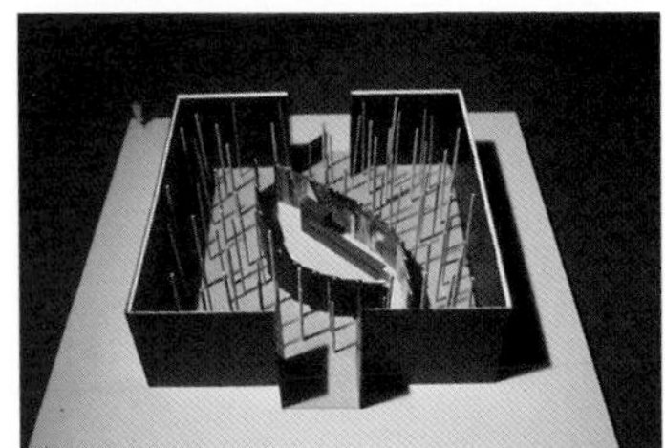

Model

This pavilion presented an exhibition by the Valais Society of Engineers and Architects for one week in October 1994. The competition specification called for an extraordinary design. Unlike "ordinary" stands (light, 2.5 metres high, extraverted) the project proposes a dark, high, introverted mass.

The pavilion is designed as an installation where only the space is presented, in order to make it a memorable place. This space is by its nature ephemeral. It borrows from the building site a means of implementation intended to be reused: a system of formwork (girders, shuttering and stays).

From the outside, the pavilion presents a dark, smooth skin. Inside, the main space is designed as a dark place lit by small openings cut in the interior skin and structured by the stayed "masts", which are not squared. The walls are scattered with slides provided by all the members of the society. In the central (light) space there are people waiting to welcome visitors and to give the more curious of them further information about the society's aims and activities. The whole construction system and lighting can be hired (assembly, hire, dismantling) for trade fairs. Only some of the shuttering panels with cut-outs and the V60 slate floor cannot be re-used.

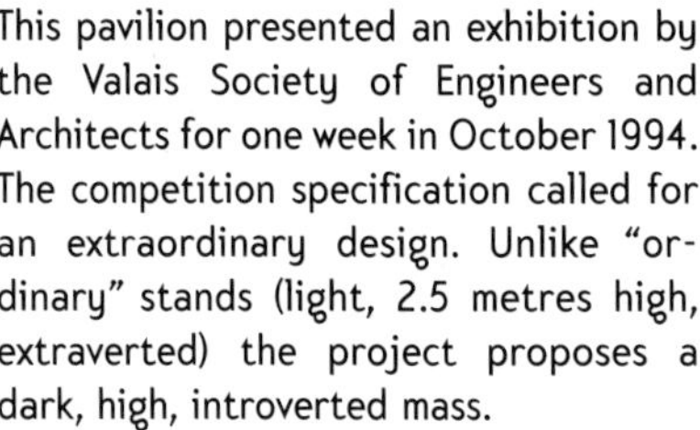

Forest, prefabricated framework and stays

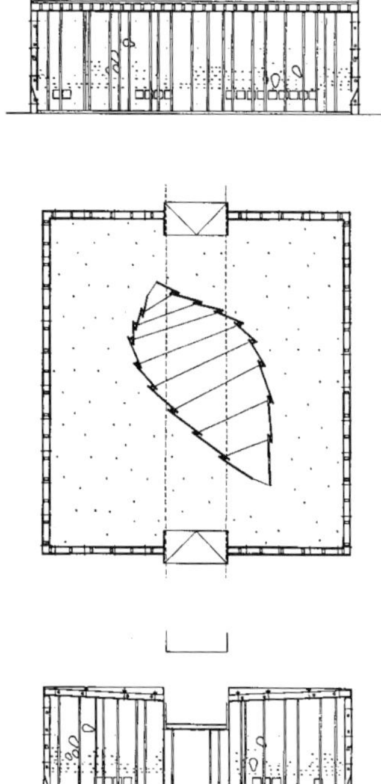

Plan and sections

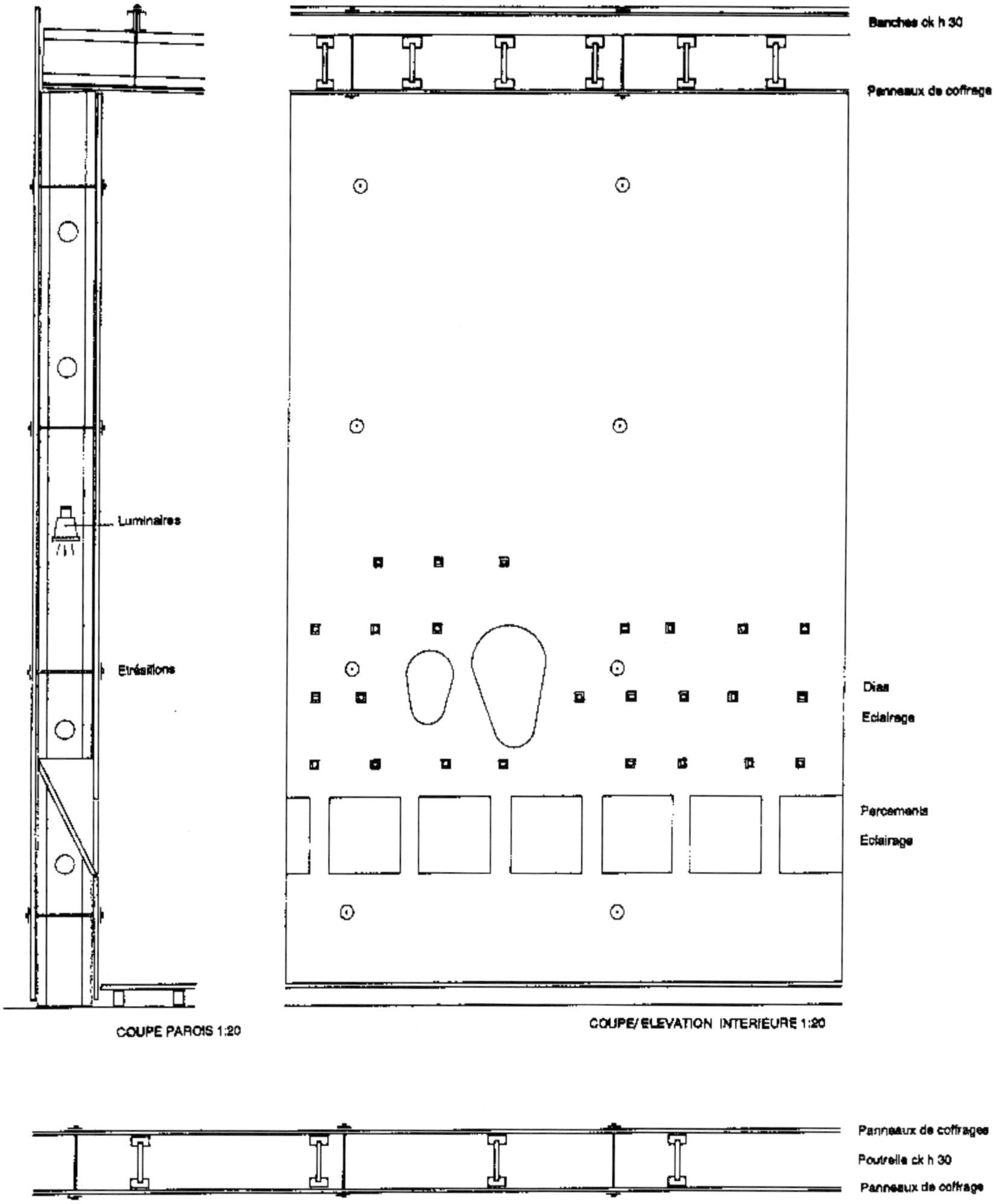

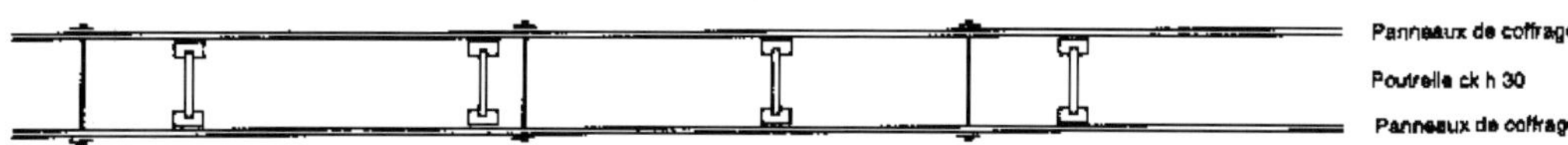

Construction detail

Taking up

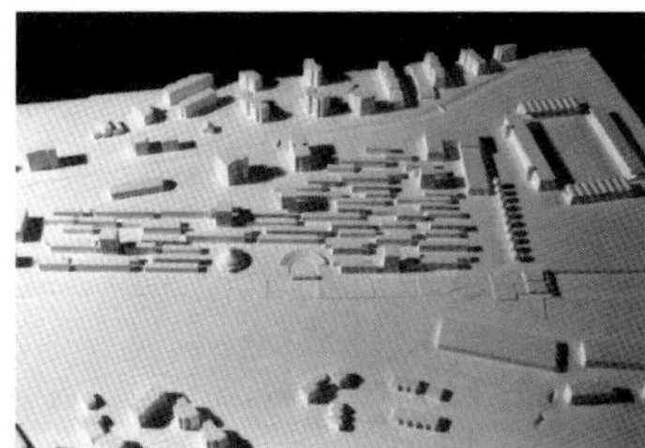

The project proposes the erection of an ephemeral structure for the duration of the Olympic Games to take 70 per cent of the Olympic village buildings.

To build the Olympic village accommodation using standard modern prefabricated parts and reusing them after the Olympic games to meet modern

built using a standard system of wooden anti-noise sections. It is intended that these will be reused as anti-noise screens (railway, road, motorway, etc.).

Constructional and energy concept: The system of wooden anti-noise walls, and a system with frame and infill panels

"Accommodation for 3,500 people

day requirements, in particular the anti-noise sections (walls, floor, facades) and prefabricated sanitary units (renovation of old buildings).

The facades, floors and inner walls of the ephemeral accommodation are

are designed to resist even the most severe climatic conditions.

Insulation that guarantees noise absorption also satisfies the thermic requirements for the accommodation during the Games.

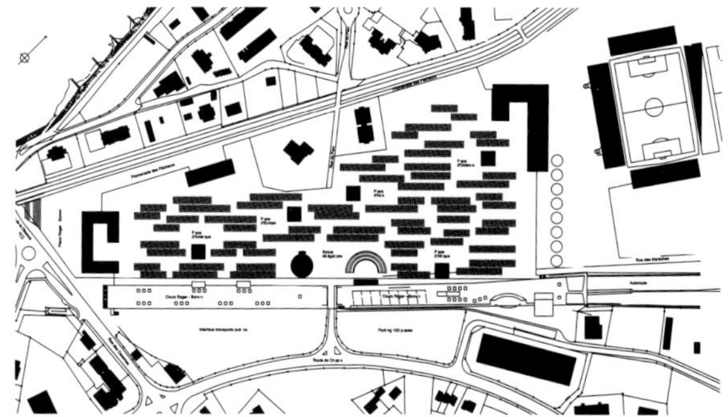

Plan de situation

This wooden construction (renewable and recyclable) requires much less production energy than a traditional solid structure (panels 400 MJ/m^2 rather than 1000 MJ/m^2).

The Olympic village, like the villages of the Valais, is composed of very densely arranged two to three-storey wooden

= 37km noise-reduction screen"

buildings. From inside the village, only the relationships with the peaks of the mountains and with Valère and Tourbillon are preserved and brought into the scene.

The five permanent buildings house the technical structures for the village.

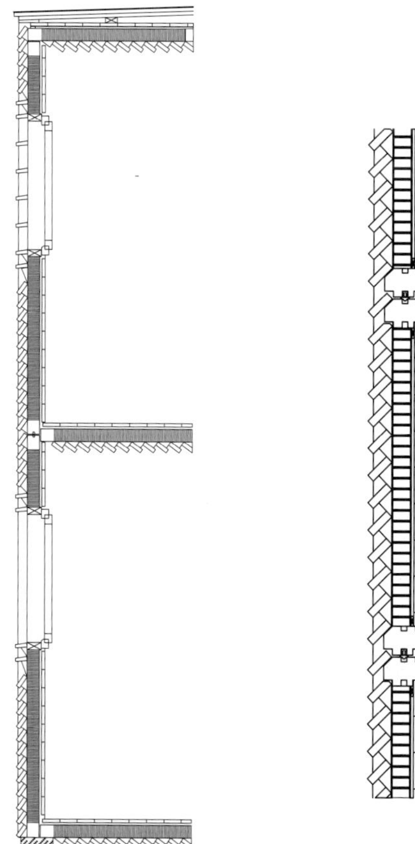

Construction detail

Today the SNL is part of a dense network of town, canton and university
libraries. Access to information has
changed profoundly for every citizen,
and the internet will reinforce the efficiency of the network by bringing the
information directly into the heart of
every home. The role delegated to the
network will be that of distribution of
the information. Only those documents
not accessible through other channels
will need to be held at the SNL for consultation.

Ever since they began, libraries have
been evolving in response to technical
developments such as the birth of
printing, or political developments such
as freedom of access, with the storage
areas being increasingly separated
from the reading areas. This separation
will become more marked with the
development of digital technologies,
the screen already being the most com-
monly used interface for consulting
catalogues or ordering documents.

In the face of this culture of the ephemeral, the role of the SNL must recentre
itself around its specific tasks of collection and long-term preservation.

Exhibition: flipbook

Extract from the flipbook

Conservation strategies

How does one tackle the problem of the perpetuity of a trace over time? From the architect's point of view, history offers us two different paths.
These two methods could form the basis of a conservation strategy that takes account of the fundamentally different characters of traditional trace media and digital media. The first type, based on the physical permanence of the media, requires the provision of ideal climatic conditions for the perpetuity of the original document: constant hygrometry and temperature. The second takes account of the continuous development of media and the ways in which digital documents are accessed by regularly renewing them.

Architecture cannot provide an answer as to how the information will be accessed and distributed; this will depend on digital technologies. **On the other hand, it must provide a lasting solution to the questions of conservation of the documents and limitless growth of the stock.**

Safeguarding through permanence

1 Edfu temple, Egypt

Perpetuity is guaranteed by the combination of simple construction principles and climatic conditions.

Safeguarding through renewal

2 Temple of Ise, Japan

Ever since its foundation the temple has been rebuilt every 21 years, exactly as it was before. The building is destroyed before any trace of degradation has appeared, to make room for an identical edifice. The principle of reconstruction in identical form calls the traditional notion of originality into question.

3 Grain store principle

Faced with the problems of "instantaneous" distribution and "eternal" conservation of documents, the plan proposes a radical separation of these areas, which are governed by completely opposing temporal realities:

- An interface building accommodating the latest technical refinements. Its infrastructure will be in constant evolution, adapting itself according to the practices and methods of each successive generation. Since the present Swiss National Library building does not have the scope to absorb the mass of documents to come in the future, this urban edifice could become this interface, which would receive the public and collect and process documents.

- A timeless storage infrastructure that spans the generations, while guaranteeing the permanence required by the constitutional aims of the SNL. This must be positioned close to a hub of physical and digital communications to ensure fast and efficient interaction with the interface building.

This infrastructure must guarantee permanent ideal climatic conditions for the conservation of documents and must meet the continual growth of the mass of documents to be conserved.

4 Cellar principle

Plan: library with unlimited growth

The combination of these archetypes (the cellar and the grain store) makes it possible to construct a space guaranteeing constant hygrometry and temperature but not requiring an energy supply or the continual maintenance inherent to technical climate control installations.

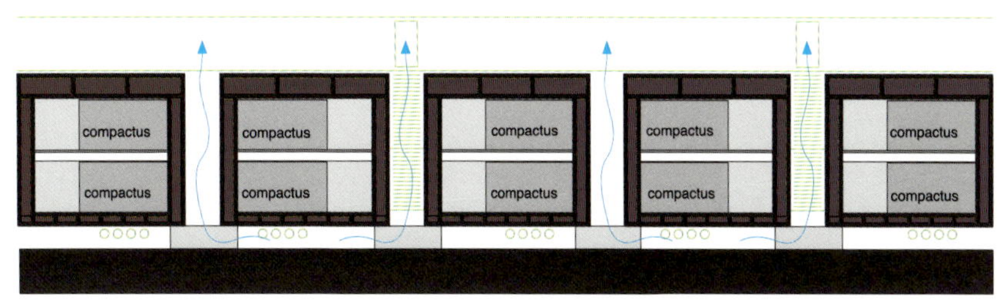

Notional part section

Coupled with natural ventilation, the vast mass of a conglomeration of expanded stone and clay cement guarantees constant temperature and hygrometry. The technical installations are designed as non-essential ephemeral complements relating to the particular requirements of each generation.

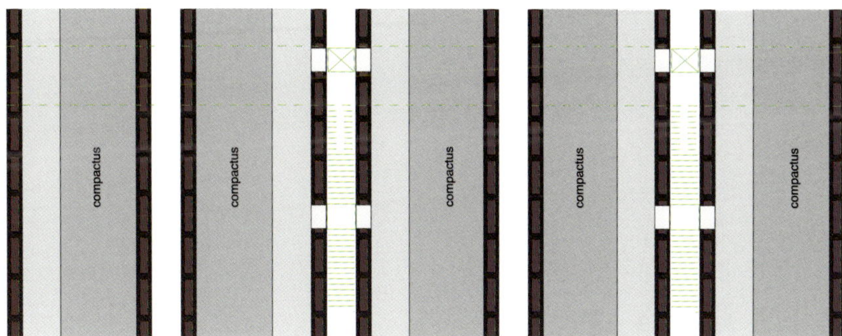

Notional plan

The stock access installations are designed as technical elements renewable according to the practices and methods of each generation. The stock is organised mainly chronologically, while the IT catalogues allow categorisation by every imaginable subject area.

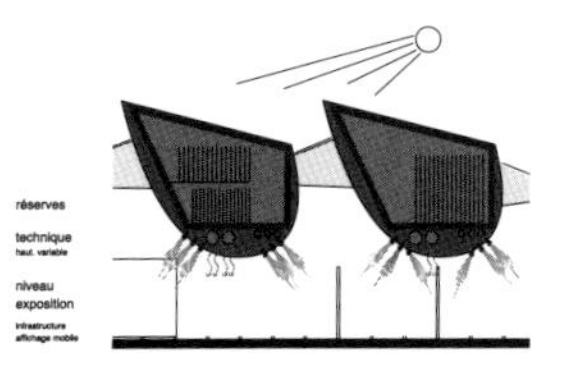

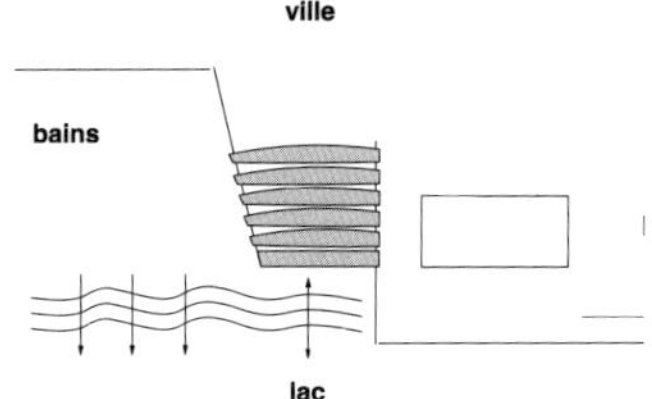

The museum: an infrastructure combining the permanence required to preserve the works of art with the flexibility of the exhibition spaces. The project proposes a synthesis of these needs by literally constructing the exhibition space through the installation of the preservation areas.

The construction of the storage infrastructure is based on a revisiting of ancestral methods of conserving perishable produce: the grain store (guaranteeing the absence of dampness) and the cellar (guaranteeing a constant temperature). The combination of these archetypes makes it possible to build a space guaranteeing constant hygrometry and temperature, with low energy requirements. The material required to create the desired thermal inertia also forms the structure that frees the large exhibition halls from any supporting columns, giving these exhibition interfaces the necessary flexibility to adapt to the museographical developments of successive generations.

In the interstice between two infrastructures positioned back to back (the swimming baths and the ports) the project seeks in the first place to create a relationship with the town and the lake. However, the elements that form the character of these neighbouring structures find their echo in the project, whether this be in the building's relationship with the lake or through its naval character, which is in keeping with the spirit of the surrounding area.

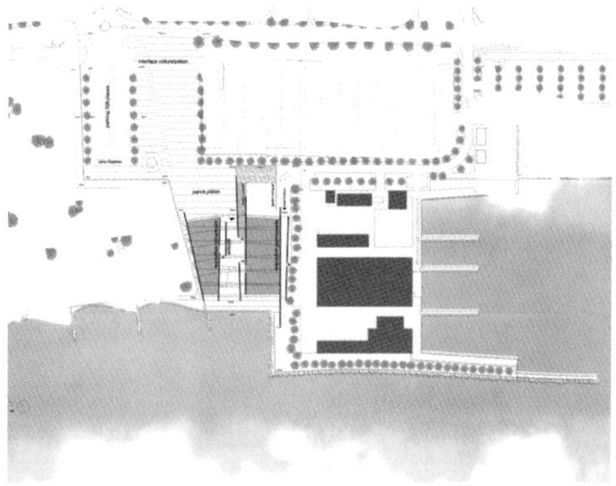

Site plan

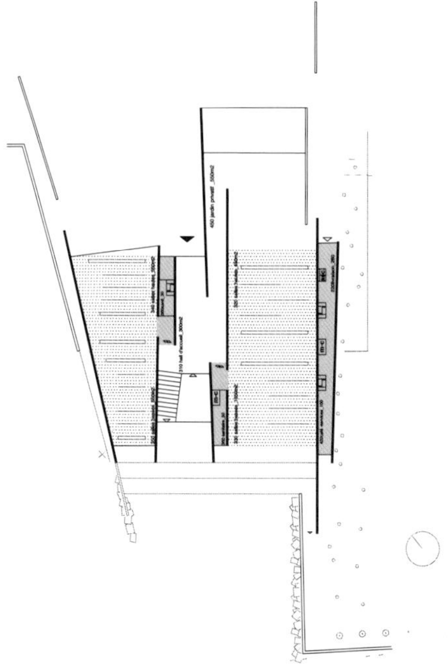

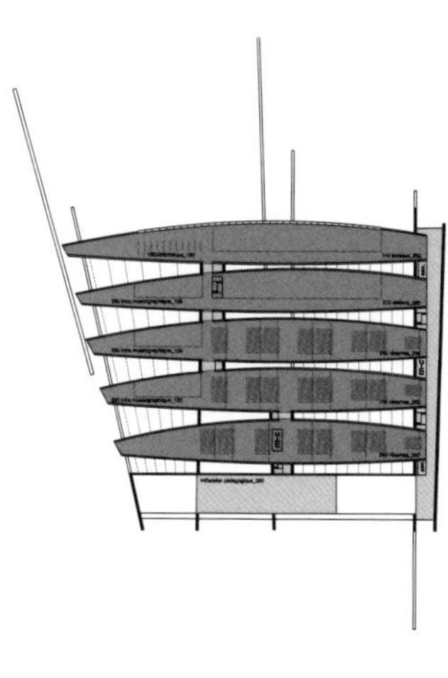

Entrance level plan

Stocking level plan

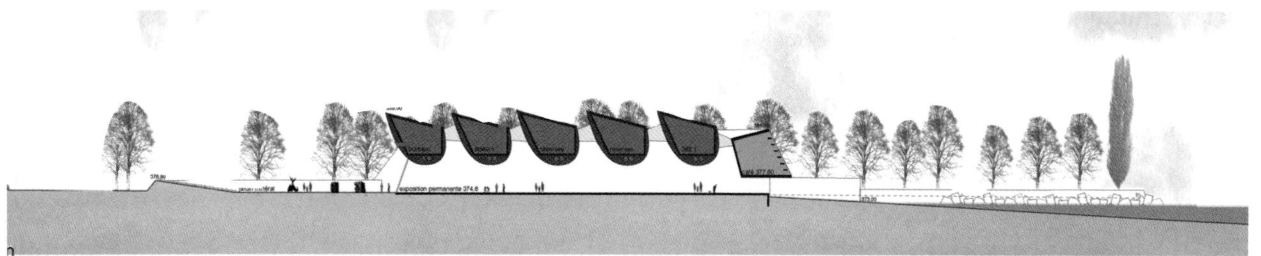

Long section

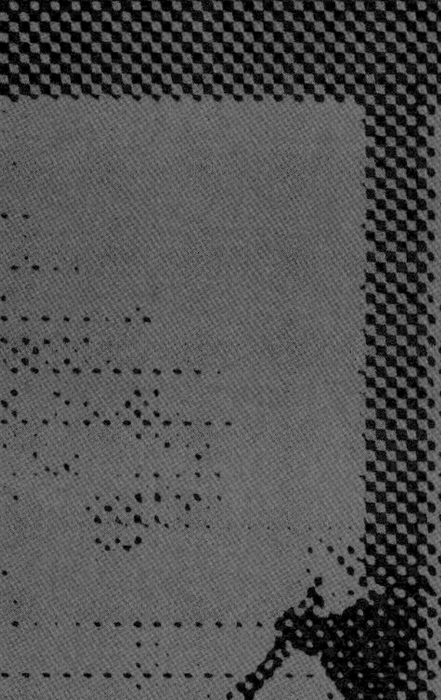

Taking stock

Olivier Galletti's Final Diploma Project
Collombey Quarry regeneration
Professor: Martin Steinman
Assistant: Jean-Luc Grobéty
Expert: Marie-Claude Betrix, April 1989

Claude Matter's Final Diploma Project
Renens Railway Station square regeneration
Professor: Luigi Snozzi
Assistants: Pierre-Alain Croset and Jean-Luc Rayon
Expert: Marie-Claude Betrix, April 1989

1. Two family house,
Lausanne (vd), project 1987, realisation 1992
Won the 1993 prize for best use of concrete, "la distinction vaudoise d'architecture" and Palladio prize 1993

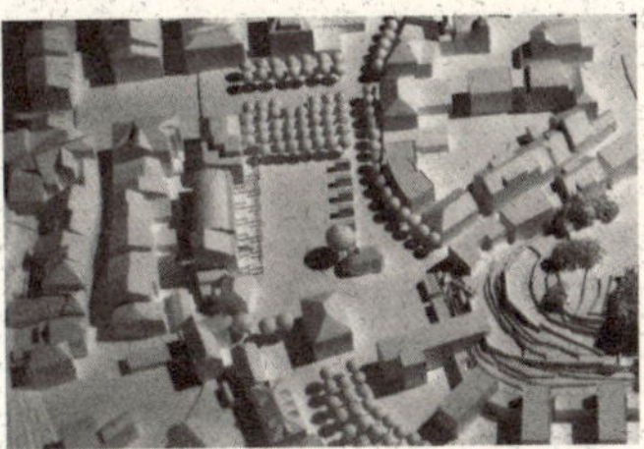

2. Town hall square
Conseil chambers and parking
Monthey (vs), competition 1989, 1st prize

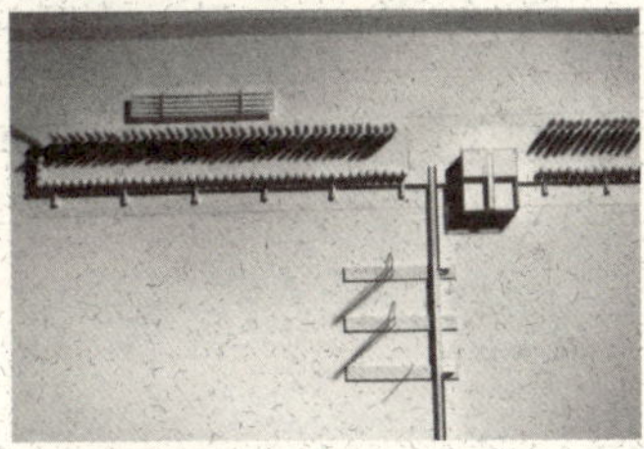

3. Motorway stop Martigny
Martigny (vs), competition 1989, 4th prize

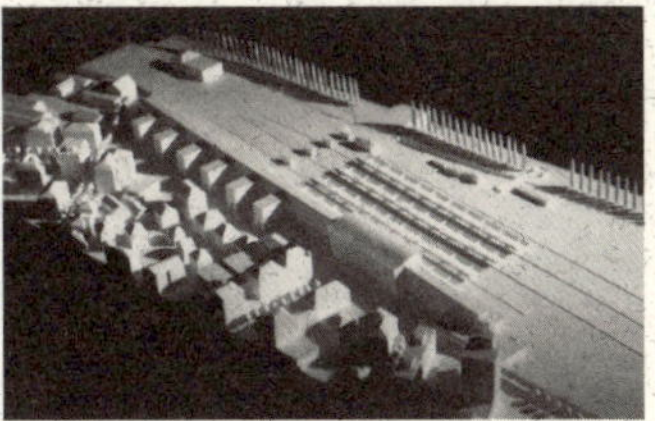

4. Brig railway station
Brig (vs), competition 1989

5. Single family house
Collombey (vs), project 1989,
realisation 1990

6. Cantonal sports centre
Steg (vs), competition 1990

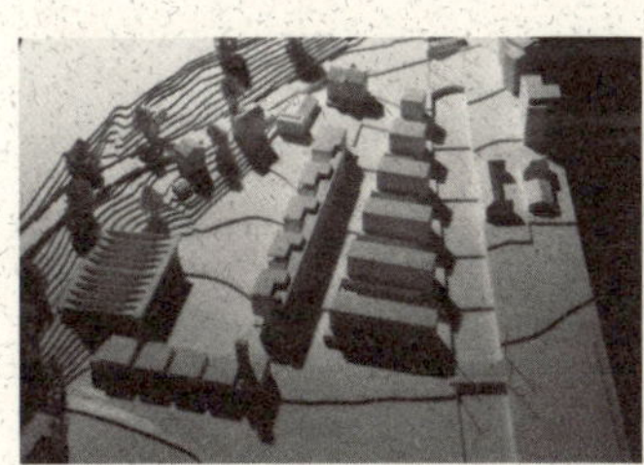

7. School complex with fire service
Monthey (vs),
competition in collaboration with
Yves Jacot 1990, 2nd prize

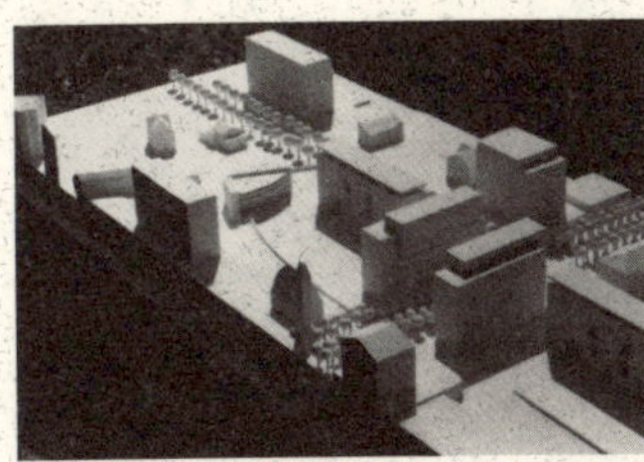

8. Restructuring proposal
av. de l'Europe – av. de la Gare,
Monthey (vs), outline planning study, 1990

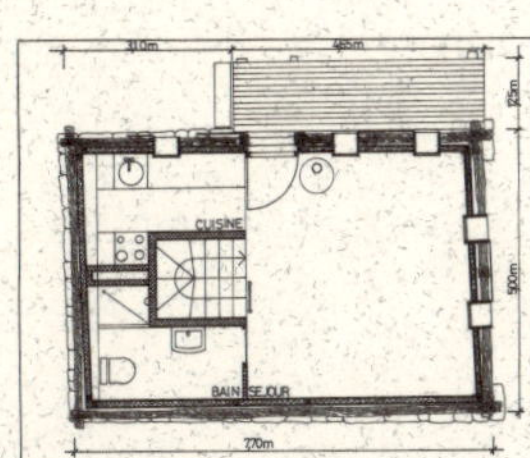

9. Conversion on an Alpine Chalet
Vernamiège (vs), project 1990,
realisation 1991

10. School complex, Vercorin (vs),
competition 1991

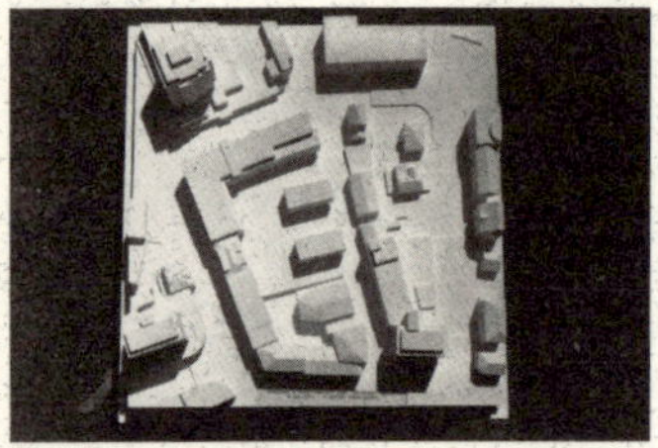

11. Urban restructuring proposal
«îlot Neyroudaz» Monthey (vs),
project 1991, 1st prize

12. New landscape proposal for
«La Croire» Quarry
Collombey (vs), competition 1991

13. School and gymnasium hall
Fully (vs), competition in collaboration
with Jacqueline Pittet and Blaise Tardin,
1st prize, realisation 1995

14. Communal sports centre «aux îles»
Yverdon-les-Bains (vd), competition 1991

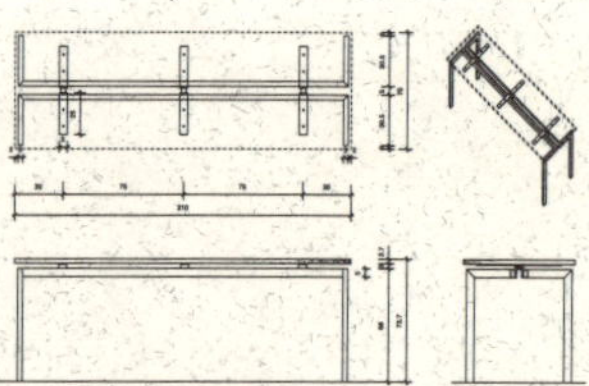

15. Long span table
project and realisation 1992

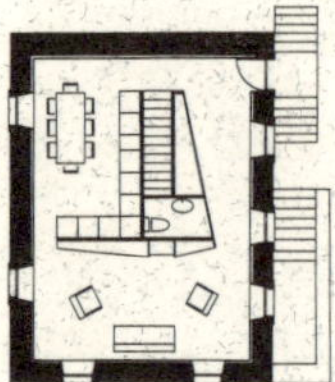

16. Hut conversion
Puidoux (vd), project 1992

17. Primary school and gymnasium hall
Rarogne (vs), competition in collaboration
with Yves Jacot 1992, 4th prize

18. Renovation of a house
La Chaux-de-Fonds (ne),
project and built 1992

19. Ice-rink and exhibition centre Espace
Gruyère
Bulle, competition in collaboration with
Yves Jacot 1993, 1st prize, realisation 1998

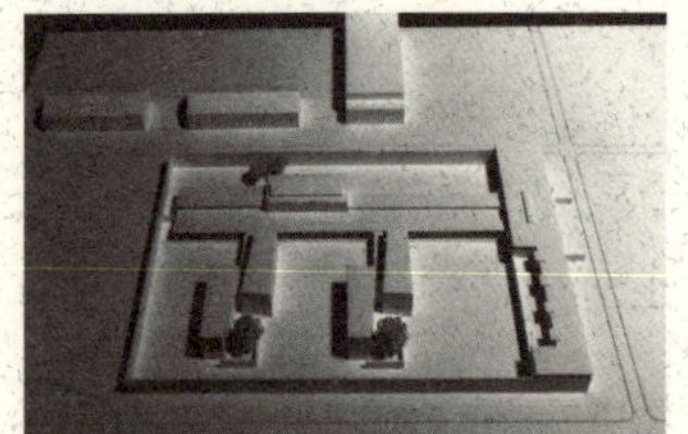

20. Cantonal prison
Sion (vs), competition 1993, 4th prize

21. EPFL North-sector Ecublens
Lausanne (vd), competition in collaboration
with Christine Thibault-Zingg, Jean-Luc
Thibault and Nicole Maeder 1993

22. School for computer studies and
tourism
Sierre (vs), competition 1993, 4th prize

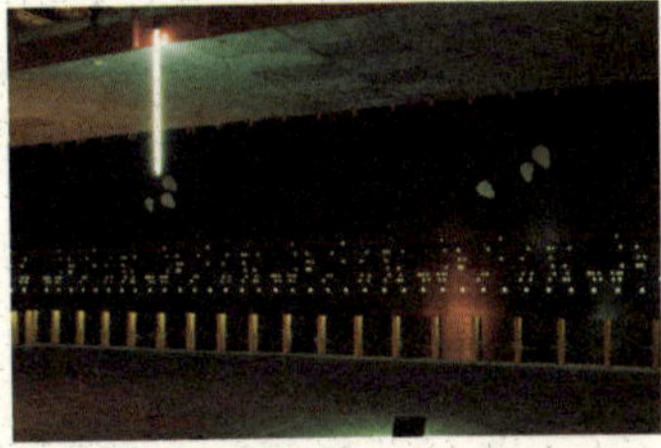

23. SIA pavilion
Martigny (vs), competition 1994, 1st prize,
constructed and dismounted in 1994

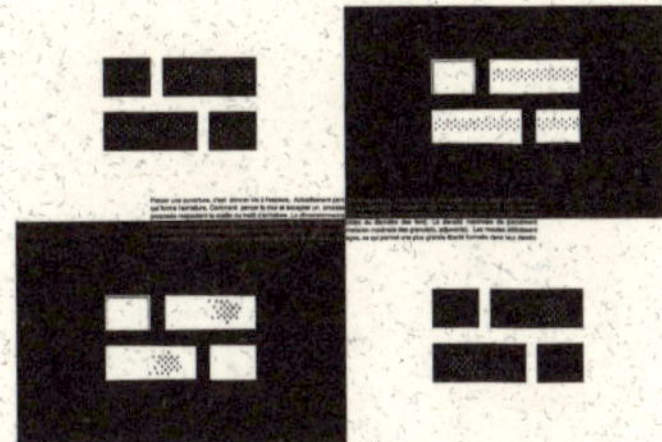

24. Prefabricated garages
BTR (Prébéton), competition 1994, 3rd prize

25. Single family house
Bex (vd), project 1994, realisation 1995

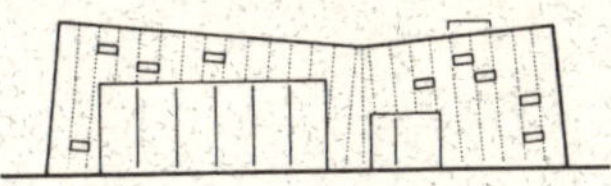

26. Ministry of transport depot
Evionnaz, outline planning study 1994

27. Studio conversion for the centre for
professional teaching North Vaud
Yverdon (vd), competition in collaboration
with Jacqueline Pittet and Blaise Tardin

28. Alpine chalet conversion
Sarreyer (vs), project 1995, realisation 1996

29. Conversion of three apartment house
Lausanne (vd), project 1995,
realisation 1996

30. Psychiatric care centre, north-sector
Yverdon-les-Bains (vd), competition 1995

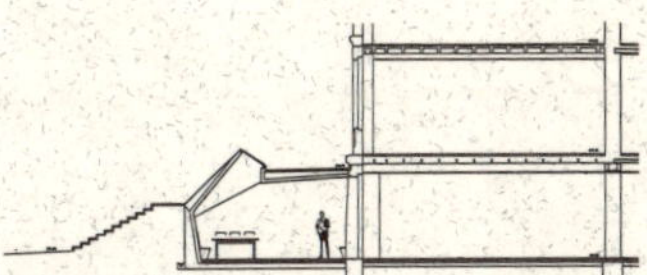

31. Cafeteria extension
Gymnasium Bugnon
Lausanne (vd), outline planning study 1995,
1st prize

32. Motorway stop
Bavois (vd), competition 1995

33. Single family house
Lausanne (vd), project 1996

34. Civil protection shelter and sports hall
Vufflens-la-Ville (vd), outline planning
study 1996

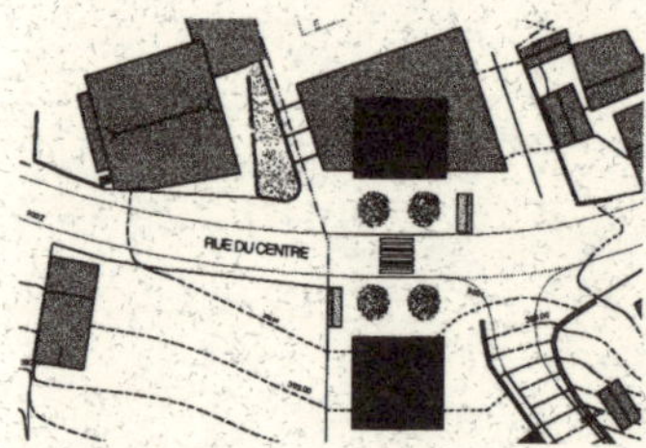

35. College of professional and superior education
Marcelin Morges (vd), competition in collaboration with Jacqueline Pittet and Blaise Tardin 1996, 2nd prize

36. Council buildings
Saint-Sulpice (vd), competition 1996

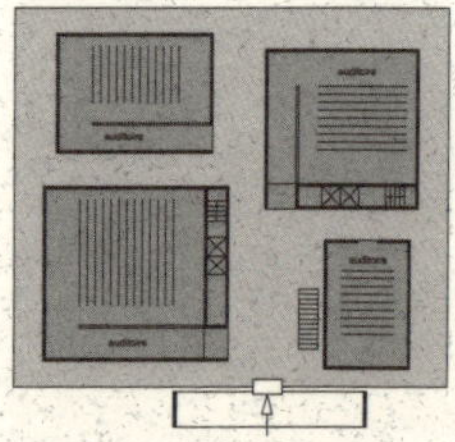

37. School complex «En Bresse»
Vétroz (vs), competition 1996

38. Fribourg university
«Plateau de Pérolles»
Fribourg (fr), competition 1997

39. Alpine restaurant and rooms
Längfluh Saas-Fee (vs), competition 1997, 6th prize

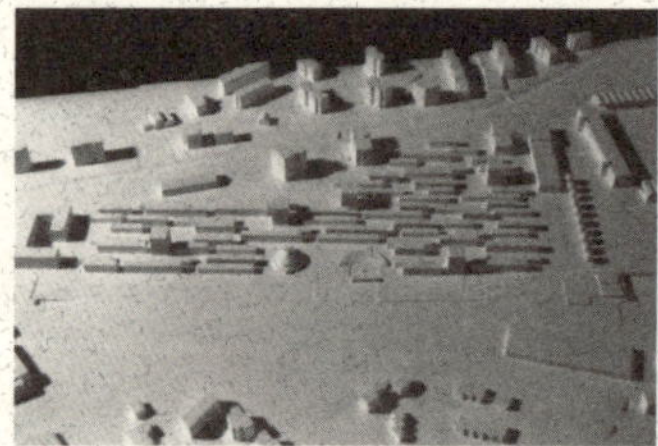

40. Middle school
Collombey-Muraz (vs), competition 1997, 1st prize, realisation 1997/98

41. Olympic village study
Sion (vs), competition 1997

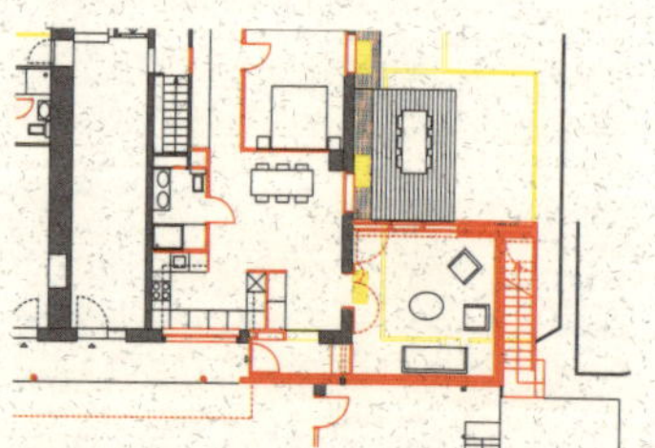

42. Dwelling of the future
Delémont (ju), competition 1998

43. Renovation of a housing block
Collombey (vs), project 1998, realisation 1998/99

44. Traffic circle development
Carouge (ge), outline planning study 1998

45. School complex extension and station area redesign
Port-Valais, Bouveret (vs), competition 1998

46. School complex «Vers-l'église»
Fully (vs), competiton 1998

47. School complex
Plan-Conthey (vs), competition 1998,
6th prize

48. Leisure and sports centre «En Boulay»
Romont (fr), competition 1998, 3rd prize

49. Market square regeneration
Bulle (fr), competition in collaboration with
A3 1999, 1st prize

50. Hôtel Guisan
Berne (be), outline planning study 1999

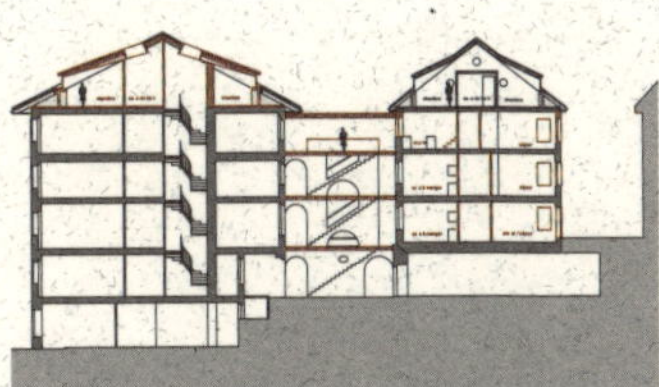

51. Apartment building conversion
Place de la Palud 21-25 bis, Lausanne (vd),
outline planning study 1999

52. College and infant school complex
with gymnasium hall
Pully-nord (vd), competition 1999

53. School complex «La Tambourine»
Carouge (ge), competition 1999, 3rd prize

54. School complex Tombay II
Bussigny-près-Lausanne (vd),
competition 1999

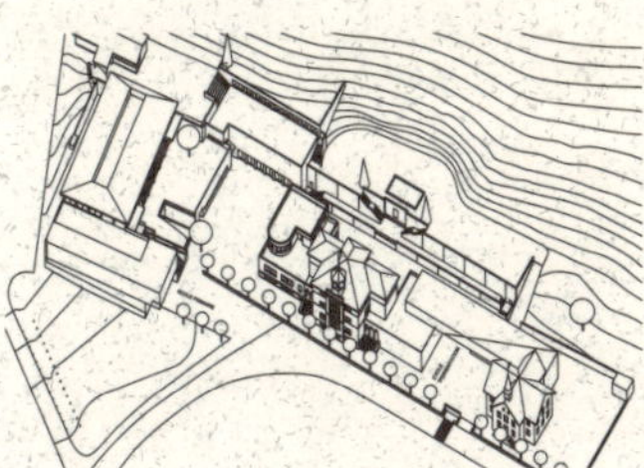

55. Middle school extension
Grône (vs), competition 1999

56. Middle school Gruyère
La Tour-de-Trême (fr), competition 1999

57. Infant school with extension to the
high school «Des Buttes»
Rolle (vd), competition in collaboration
with Julien Grisel 1999, 3rd prize

58. Middle school development
Gibloux, Farvagny (fr), competition 1999

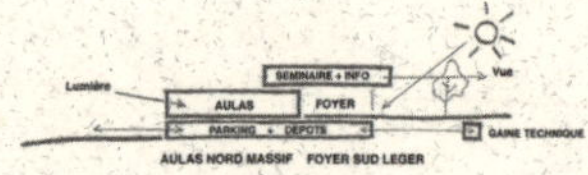

59. Lecture halls for the university of Lausanne-Dorigny
Lausanne (vd), competition 2000

60. Multi-use hall and sportsground
Grône (vs), competition 2000

61. Medical clinic conversion
Neuchâtel (ne), project and realisation 2000

62. Local infrastructure and social services complex
Nyon (vd), competition 2000, 1st prize

63. Extension of the «Ecole d'études sociales et pédagogiques»
Lausanne (vd), competition 2000, 2nd prize

64. Regional funeral centre,
Nyon (vd), competition 2000

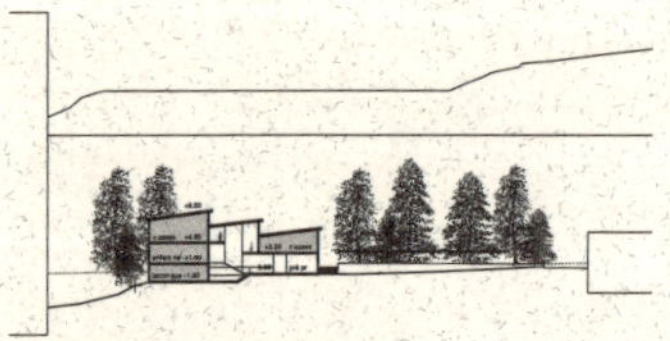

65. High school in Villars
Ollon (vd), competition 2000

66. House conversion
Chexbres (vd), project and realisation 2000

67. Sports and multi-use hall
Renens (vd), competition 2000, 1st prize, realisation 2002

68. Phoniatric and logopedical unit, CHUV
Lausanne (vd), outline planning study 2000, 1st prize, realisation 2004

69. Primary school extension
Saillon (vs), outline planning study 2000, 1st prize, realisation 2002

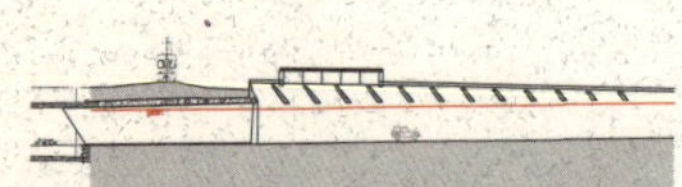

70. A 201 motorway tunnel, Sous-le-Scex
Sion (vs), competition 2000

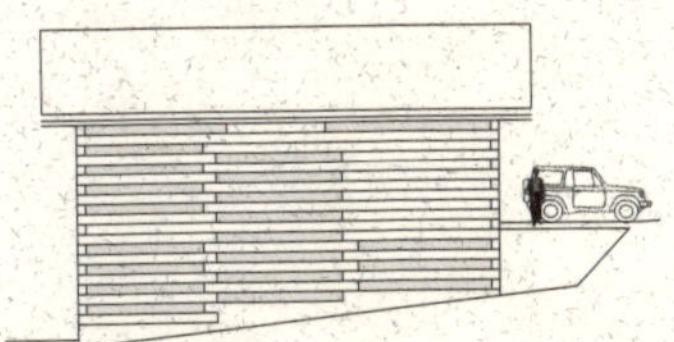

71. Chalet single family
Champéry (vs), project 2000

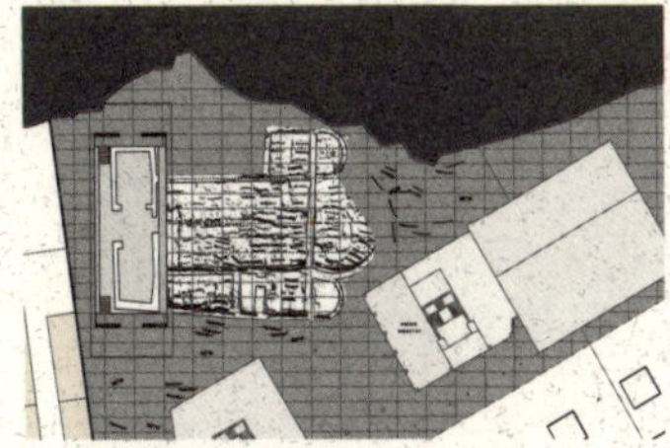

72. Revalorisation and conservation
of the funeral Basilica
Sion (vs), outline planning study 2001

73. Swiss National Library project
Berne (be), outline planning study 2001

74. Multi-use hall and library
Collombey-Muraz (vs), outline planning
study 2001, 1st prize, realisation 2003

75. Concert hall and casino «Le Scex»
Sion (vs), competition 2001, 1st prize

76. Kitchen renovation
Les Diablerets (vd),
project and realisation 2001

77. Middle school
Bellinzona (ti), competition 2001

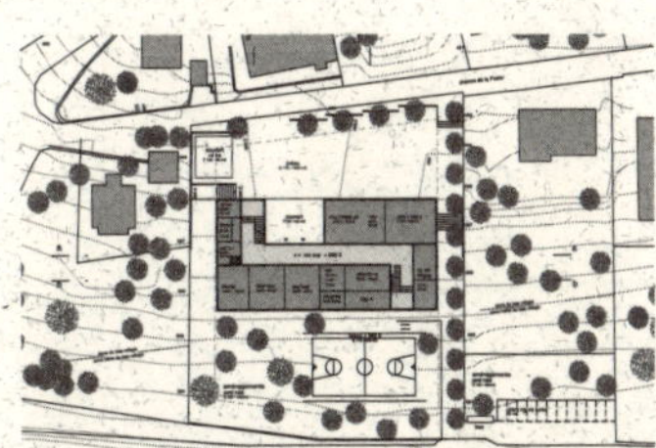

78. School «Pressoirs»
Lonay (vd), competition 2001

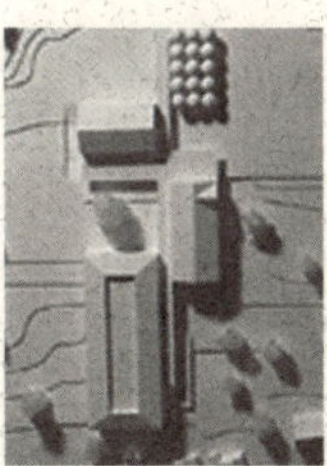

79. College and gymnasium hall
Cugy (vd), competition 2001

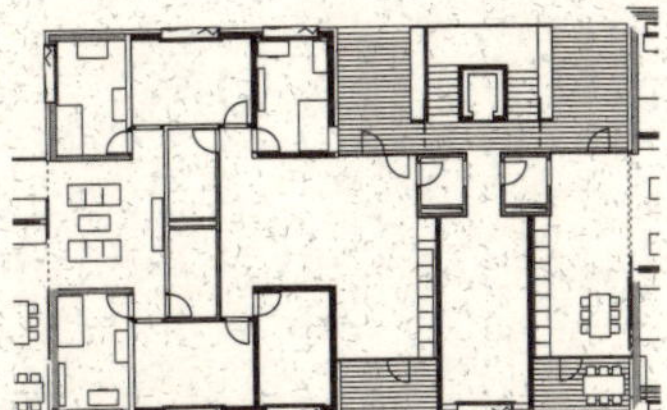

80. Residential buildings Bernerstrasse
Zürich-Altstetten (zh), competition 2001

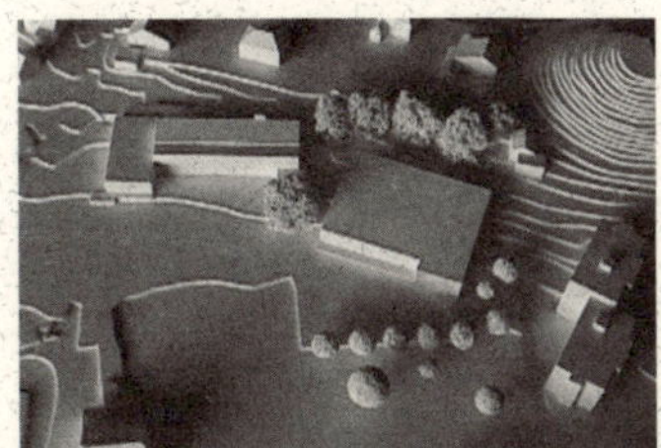

81. Primary school «Muriers»
Colombier (ne), competition 2002

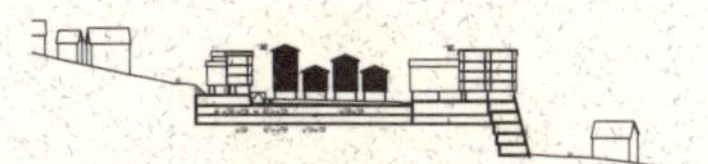

82. Site layout «Médran»
Verbier (vs), outline planning study 2002

83. School and sports complex Bahyse
Blonay (vd), competition 2002

84. Loft conversion
Lausanne (vd), project 2002,
realisation 2003

85. Village centre with gymnasium hall
and multi-use hall
Lavigny (vd), outline planning study in
collaboration with Urbaplan 2002

86. House
Les Cullayes (vd), project 2003

87. High school «La Carrière»
Crissier (vd), competition 2003, 1st prize,
currently under construction

88. Development of square «Pré de Foire»
Martigny-Bourg (vs), competition 2003,
2nd prize

89. School complex renovation
Renens (vd), outline planning study in
collaboration with Astrid Dettling and
Jean-Marc Péléraux 2003, 1st prize

90. Middle school extension «Goubing»
Sierre (vs), competition 2003

91. Village centre with multi-use hall and
shopping facilities
Ballaigues (vd), outline planning study 2003

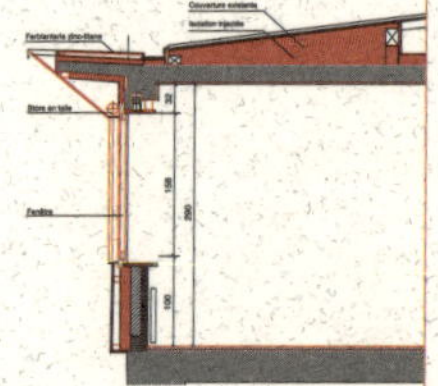

92. Lausanne school for professional
studies
Lausanne (vd), 2004

93. Single family house
Fully (vs), project 2004

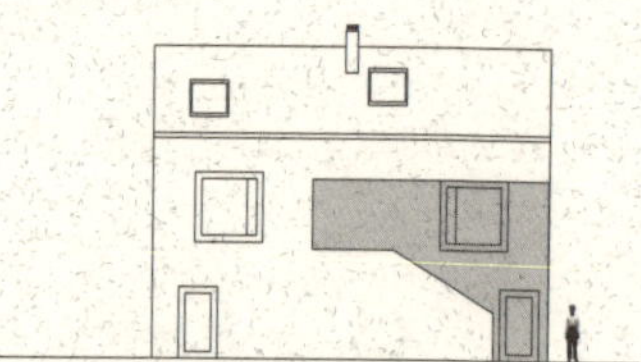

94. Single family house
Bremblens (vd), project 2004

95. Village council service and public depot
Bremblens (vd), competition 2004

96. New museum of modern art
Lausanne (vd), competition 2004

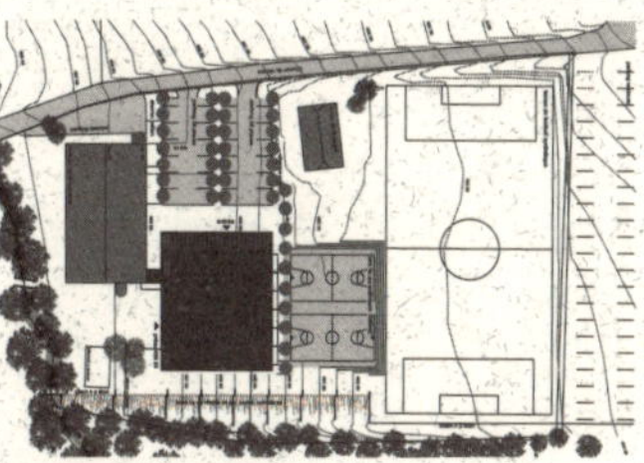

97. Sports hall for the international
school of Geneva
Founex (vd), competition 2004

98. School and gymnasium hall extension
Val D'Illiez (vs), outline planning study 2004

99. Transformation of the school of
chemistry into the college of health
Lausanne (vd), competition 2004, 1st prize

100. Galletti & Matter, collection of
places, buildings & projects
Birkhäuser Publishers, Basel 2005

Awards for completed works

The buildings are to be considered in a spatial context of time and use.
We are constantly searching for specific answers to each problem.
Numerous prizes and awards confirm the spirit of innovation which is nurtured in our offices.

Vaudoise award in Achitecture 1992
International Andrea Palladio prize 1993
Swiss award for best use of concrete 1993
Die Beste Architektur, 10 vor 10/Hochparterre 1998: Silberner Hase

Exhibitions - TV reports

1992   Achitectural portraits – Lausanne Vaud
1993   Premio Internationale di Architettura Andrea Palladio Vicenza
1994   Zaragoza Architecture Bienniale
1994   Swiss Federal Institute of Technology, Lausanne-Zürich,
        prize for best use of concrete
1994   Bauten junger internationaler Architekten, Fontane Haus Berlin
1998   The Swiss Romande exists: TV report by the Swiss public television
2001   Swiss Architectour Galletti and Matter Architects; TV report by the Swiss
        public television

Main publications

"Architektur der französischen Schweiz", in *Baumeister*, no. 1, 1990.

Inès Lamunière, Pierre Devanthéry, "Tout béton, tout bois, oui mais... Deux réalisations de Brauen & Waelchli et de Galletti & Matter", in *Faces*, no. 25, 1992.

"Une maison conçue comme un paysage. Deux appartements formant une habitation, Lausanne" in *Portraits d'architecture Vaudoise 1989–1991*, Editions Payot Lausanne, 1992.

Olivier Galletti, Claude Matter, "Habitations Lausanne", in *archithese*, no. 4, 1993.

"Casa bifamiliare a Losanna" in *Premio Internationale di Architettura Andrea Palladio*, Milan, 1993.

"Deux habitations, chemin du Languedoc, Lausanne" in *Prix d'architecture béton 93*, Verein Schweizerischer Zement-Kalk- und Gips-Fabrikanten, Zurich, 1993.

Lore Kelly, "Logik der Funktion", in *Raum und Wohnen*, no. 4, 1994.

Catherine Dumont D'Ayot, "Exposition – Pavillon SIA de la Foire du Valais 1994", in *Faces*, no. 33, 1994.

Renate Strobel, "Licht Bilder", in *Leonardo*, no. 2, 1995.

Olivier Galletti, Claude Matter, "Schule und Turnhalle in Fully", in *archithese*, no. 2, 1996.

Patrick Devanthéry, "Trois écoles, aucun modèle", in *Faces*, no. 41, 1997.

Martin Tschanz, "Sensibler Umgang mit dem Ort", in *Neue Zürcher Zeitung*, Zurich, 3.10.1997.

"La romandie existe. Das Buch, der Film", in *Hochparterre*, no. 9, 1998.

Roderick Hönig, Benedikt Loderer, "Espace Gruyère, Marché au bétail et Patinoire" in *La romandie existe. Un guide de l'architecture contemporaine*, Verlag Hochparterre, Zurich, 1998.

Roderick Hönig, "Die Besten Architektur", in *Hochparterre*, no. 12, 1998.

Olivier Galletti, Claude Matter, "Zwischen Weinberg und Felswand", in *Werk, Bauen + Wohnen*, no. 12, 1998.

Roderick Hönig, "Für Kuhhandel und Kufenakrobaten", in *Hochparterre*, no. 9, 1999.

"Schweiz –, Sinnlich und selbstbewusst. Bauen auf Schweizer Art: Portraits und Werke prominenter und aufstrebender Architekten", in *Architektur & Wohnen*, spécial issue, 1999.

"Espace Gruyère, complexe polyvalent, Bulle", in *Werk, Bauen + Wohnen*, no. 1/2, 2000.

"Drinnen. Draussen. Ein Schulhaus in Collombey, Wallis", in *Bauwelt*, no. 10, 2000.

Gilles Davoine, "Ecole secondaire, Collombey, Suisse", in *amc*, no. 105, 2000.

"Schulgebäude in Collombey, ch", in *DBZ Deutsche Bauzeitschrift*, no. 3, 2000.

"School building in Collombey", in *a+t*, no. 15, 2000.

Maya Huber, Thomas Hildebrand, "Espace Gruyère", "School Fully" in *Switzerland. A guide to recent architecture*, Ellipsis, London, 2001.

"Escuela, Collombey", in *AV monografias*, no. 89, 2001.

Frank Kaltenbach (Ed.), "Translucent Materials", Detail Praxis, Birkhäuser/Im Detail, Basel/München, 2003.

Julien Grisel, "Salle de sport à Renens", in *Faces*, no. 54, 2004.

Julien Grisel, "Des pièges à lumière", in *abstract*, no. 13, 2004.

"Extension de l'école primaire, 1913 Saillon", in *AS architecture suisse*, no. 155–154, 2004.

Carol Maillard, "25 halles de marché", "Volumes imbriqués en Suisse", in *amc*, édition du Moniteur, Paris 2004.

List of main collaborators

Meulemans Nils
Piccolo Déborah

List of other collaborators

Bétrisey Claudia - Berchtold Lukretia - Billamboz Marc - Broillet Baptiste - Cauderay Pierre - Christl Stéphane - Cisternino Davide - Clavien Delphine - Cornuz Joëlle - Costa Vanda - Couderay Pierre - Denimal Nathalie - Dessimoz Raphaël - Drygajlo Anna - Dubey Jacques - Evéquoz Grégoire - Fiorini Tomaso - Fritz Nicola - Gallatti Karin - Gaspar Iren - Gervais Chantal - Grisel Julien - Gromann Karin - Lamacchia Rino - Lecoultre Cyril - Liardet Cédric - Lutz Daniel - Mancusi Catherine - Mesa Rodrigo - Moewes Ulf - Pisoni Veruska - Remund Patrick - Renault Damien - Ribaux Sylvain - Ramos José Antonio - Rybczynska Marta - Sciarini Mara - Sharif Omar - Schwab Anne-Claire - Steeb Mariko - Steiner Philippe - Turin Laurent - Vidal José Manuel - Wyss Jean-Daniel